Going Places

Are you looking for some useful touring suggestions? Are you at a loss for things to see and do with the children? Then look no further. Here in this guide we point you in the right direction to hundreds of exciting holiday attractions in all parts of Wales. Get out and about with our suggested tours to the wealth of attractions — to the mighty mediaeval castles and historic places, to the massive slate caverns and simulated coal mines, to fascinating museums and craft workshops, to the super new leisure centres and country parks. Or let others do the driving on one of the 'Great Little Trains' of Wales.

Our series of tours also takes you off-the beaten-track, over moorlands and mountains to the natural attractions of Wales's landscape.

Contents

Important note

Please note that every effort has been made to ensure accuracy in this publication, but as changes in prices, services, opening times and any other information often occur after press date, it is essential to confirm all the information given direct with the establishment concerned. The Wales Tourist Board can accept no liability whatsoever for any inaccuracies or omissions, or for any matter in any way connected with or arising out of the publication of the information.

*Designed and published by Wales Tourist Board.
Copyright © 1984 Wales Tourist Board, Brunel House, 2 Fitzalan Road, Cardiff CF2 1UY. Printed in Britain by Dobson and Crowther, Llangollen.
ISBN 1 85013 001 9*

North Wales

Travelling out and about in North Wales your will find there's more than enough to see and do, whatever the weather. In this guide we have tried to include as many of the region's attractions as is possible. Obviously you cannot visit them all during your stay. But we do hope that by following one or two of our suggested tours, you and your family will get out and about to a few of them at least.

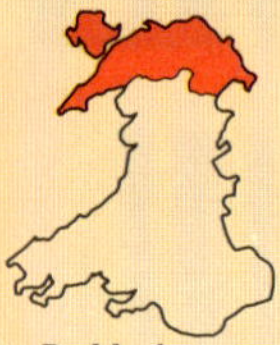

Right: Beddgelert.
Below: Llyn Ogwen in Snowdonia.
Bottom: The Llanberis Pass, in Snowdonia.

Dominating the North Wales landscape to the west is the Snowdonia mountain range, which has been attracting visitors since Victorian times. Exploring this area of lofty mountains, lakes and river valleys is quite a thrill on foot or in the comfort of a car. Mountain villages such as Llanberis, Beddgelert, Betws-y-Coed and Capel Curig make excellent touring bases. Further east the rugged, powerful landscape softens to a patchwork of forests, open moorlands, gentle hills and wooded valleys, interspersed with lovely old market towns, such as Ruthin, Llanrwst and Llangollen. Castled Denbigh, Mold and Wrexham also make convenient centres for touring this eastern corner of the region.

Down on the coast you'll find a colourful selection of seaside resorts like Colwyn Bay, Rhyl,

Below: *A splendid example of Ruthin's architecture.*

Prestatyn and Llandudno, providing plenty of activities for all the family, and so very close to dozens of holiday attractions. On the Lleyn Peninsula and the Isle of Anglesey, both areas of outstanding natural beauty, the coast is a little quieter, with hidden sandy beaches, tiny coves and rocky headlands. Even in the height of the summer season, it's always possible to find a peaceful spot.

In planning the tours of North Wales we have aimed to show you some of the region's most scenic attractions, as well as its rich heritage of mighty mediaeval castles and historic houses, its fascinating industrial sites, narrow gauge railways and museums-with a-difference, all of which are described in here.

For more detailed information about North Wales, get your copy of the Wales Tourist Board's guide to the region, featured on the back of this book. A comprehensive gazetteer of towns and villages and a useful beach guide are included. Available at leading booksellers, newsagents and information centres or direct from the *Wales Tourist Board, P.O. Box 1, Cardiff CF1 2XN.*

Below: *Llandudno Pier*
Bottom: *Take a train ride into the Llechwedd Slate Caverns at Blaenau Ffestiniog.*

Places to visit in North Wales

The following attractions are on tour routes featured in this guide.

Aberconwy House, *Conwy*
On tour 4, page 17

Beaumaris Castle
On tour 1, page 11

Beaumaris Gaol
On tour 1, page 11

Bodrhyddan Hall, *near Rhuddlan*
On tour 5, page 19

Bodnant Garden
On tour 4, page 17

Bryn Bras Castle, *Llanrug*
On tour 3, page 14

Brynkir Woollen Mill
On tour 2, page 13

Cabinlift and Tramway, Great Orme *Llandudno*
On tour 4, page 17

Caernarfon Castle & Fusiliers Museum
On tours 2 and 3, page 13

Canal Exhibition Centre, *Llangollen*
On tour 7, page 23

Chirk Castle
On tour 7, page 23

Chwarel Wynne Mine and Museum
On tour 7, page 23

Conwy Castle
On tour 4, page 17

Conwy Valley Railway Museum, *Betws-y-Coed*
On tours 3 and 4, pages 15 and 17

Denbigh Castle
On tour 5, page 19

Doll Museum, *Llandudno*
On tour 4, page 17

Dolwyddelan Castle
On tour 3, page 15

Encounter Wildlife Museum *Llanrwst*
On tour 4, page 16

Erddig Stately Home, *Wrexham*
On tour 5, page 19

Felin Isaf Flour Mill, *Glan Conwy*
On tour 4, page 16

Ffestiniog Railway
On tour 2, page 13

Golddfa Ganol Slate Mine, *Blaenau Ffestiniog*
On tour 3, page 15

Grange Cavern Military Museum *near Holywell*
On tour 5, page 19

Gwydir Castle, *Llanrwst*
On tour 4, page 16

Holywell Textile Mills
On tour 5, page 19

Llanberis Lake Railway
On tour 3, page 15

Llanfairpwll Tourist Centre
On tour 1, page 11

Llechwedd Slate Caverns, *Blaenau Ffestiniog*
On tour 3, page 15

Lloyd George Museum, *Llanystumdwy*
On tour 2, page 13

Porthmadog Maritime Museum
On tours 2 and 8, pages 13 and 25

Milestone Museum, *Bwlchgwyn*
On tour 5, page 19

Museum of Childhood, *Menai Bridge*
On tour 1, page 11

Museum of Welsh Antiquities & Art Gallery, *Bangor*
On tour 4, page 17

Penmachno—Ty Mawr Wybrnant
On tour 6, page 21

Penmachno Woollen Mill
On tour 6, page 21

Penrhyn Castle, *Bangor*
On tour 4, page 17

Plas Mawr, *Conwy*
On tour 4, page 17

Plas Newydd, *Llanfairpwll*
On tour 1, page 11

Plas Newydd, *Llangollen*
On tour 7, page 23

Rhuddlan Castle
On tour 5, page 19

Rhyl Floral Hall
On tour 5, page 18

St. Winifred's Well, *Holywell*
On tour 5, page 19

Segontium Roman Fort, *Caernarfon*
On tour 2, page 13

Snowdon Mountain Railway, *Llanberis*
On tour 3, page 15

Swallow Falls, *Betws-y-Coed*
On tour 3, page 14

Tegfryn Art Gallery, *Menai Bridge*
On tour 1, page 11

Theatr Clwyd, *Mold*
On tour 5, page 19

Valle Crucis Abbey, *Llangollen*
On tour 7, page 23

Welsh Mountain Zoo, *Colwyn Bay*
On tour 4, page 17

Welsh State Museum, *Llanberis*
On tour 3, page 15

Wylfa Nuclear Power Station
On tour 1, page 11

Mid Wales

Mid Wales is a must for motorists. Rarely will you hit upon any major hold-ups on the roads in this region, which is still relatively undiscovered by visitors. Away from the coast there are miles of quiet unspoilt mountain roads, through cool forests and man-made lakelands. Our tours of Mid Wales take you on a few of these off-the-beaten-track routes. Others take you to the well-known attractions, including the woollen mills, narrow gauge railways and craft centres of the region.

Rolling hills and often remote uplands make up the 3000 square miles of Mid Wales, which is bordered to the south by the Brecon Beacons mountain range. Dotted around this unspoilt countryside are pocket-sized market towns, which make perfect holiday touring bases. Stone-built Dolgellau is one such town, sheltering beneath the towering Cader Idris, range, yet only about half an hour's drive from the coast. From Machynlleth, Llanidloes, Rhayader and Bala there are some superb mountain roads, where you'll hardly see a car for miles, particularly if you're touring in the quieter spring or autumn months.

Sturdy stone-built Dolgellau, beneath Cader Idris

Bottom: *Aberdovey's attractive seafront.*
Below: *Market day at Machynlleth.*
Right: *A familiar scene in rural Wales.*

Newtown and Welshpool, like the smaller border towns of Knighton and Presteigne, are easy to get to from the main motorway network, and are convenient for touring the distinctive and historic Welsh Marches. Spa towns have always been renowned for their peaceful qualities and unhurried pace. The lovely old towns of Llandrindod, Llangammarch and Llanwrtyd Wells still retain that timelessness.

Mid Wales's entire coastline forms part of Cardigan Bay. Along this long, sweeping shore there are sand-duned beaches, rocky headlands, sheltered coves and a chain of small resorts and coastal villages. Aberystwyth, the largest of these resorts, has amongst its many attractions a cliff railway, a narrow gauge steam-operated railway, which runs through the wooded Rheidol Valley, and a purpose-built arts centre for all-the-year-round entertainment.

To the south is Aberaeron, noted for its gem of a harbour, and near-neighbours New Quay and Cardigan. The Cambrian Coast, to the north, offers some good beaches too, at Barmouth, Fairbourne, Tywyn and Aberdovey.

For more detailed information about Mid Wales, get your copy of the Wales Tourist Board's guide to the region, featured on the back of this book. A comprehensive gazetteer of towns and villages, and a useful beach guide are included. Available at leading booksellers, newsagents and information centres or direct from the *Wales Tourist Board, P.O. Box 1, Cardiff CF1 2XN.*

Below: *In the peaceful Dysynni Valley.*

Places to visit in Mid Wales

The following attractions are on tour routes featured in this guide.

Aberaeron Sea Aquarium
On tour 14, page 37

Aberystwyth Arts Centre
On tour 11, page 31

Aberystwyth Cliff Railway
On tour 11, page 31

Bala Lake Railway
On tours 6 and 9, pages 21 and 27

Cambrian Factory, *Llanwrtyd Wells*
On tour 13, page 35

Cardigan Wildlife Park
On tour 14, page 37

Castell-y-bere, *near Tywyn*
On tour 10, page 29

Celmi Candles, *Ffestiniog*
On tour 6, page 21

Cenarth Fishing Museum
On tour 14, page 37

Ceredigion Museum, *Aberystwyth*
On tour 11, page 31

Cilgerran Castle
On tour 14, page 37

Cymer Abbey, *Llanelltyd*
On tour 8, page 25

Devil's Bridge
On tours 11 and 13, page 30 and 35

Elan and Claerwen Dams
On tour 13, page 35

Fairbourne Railway
On tour 10, page 29

Felin Geri Flour Mill,
near Newcastle Emlyn
On tour 14, page 37

Ffestiniog Railway
On tour 2, page 13

Harlech Castle
On tour 8, page 25

Llandrindod Wells Museum
On tour 12, page 33

Llandrindod Wells Rock Park Spa
On tour 12, page 33

Llanidloes Museum
On tour 11, page 30

Llyn Clywedog
On tour 11, page 30

Llywernog Silver-Lead Mine,
Ponterwyd
On tour 11, page 30

Maes Artro Tourist Village,
Llanbedr, near Harlech
On tour 8, page 25

Maesgwm Visitor Centre
Ganllwyd
On tour 8, page 25

Maesllyn Woollen Mill and Museum
On tour 14, page 37

Meirion Mill,
Dinas Mawddwy
On tours 9 and 10, pages 27 and 29

Nanteos Stately Home,
near Aberystwyth
On tour 11, page 30

National Centre for Alternative Technology, *Corris*
On tour 10, page 29

National Library of Wales,
Aberystwyth
On tour 11, page 30

Newtown Textile Museum
On tour 12, page 33

Offa's Dyke
On tour 12, page 33

Old Llanfair Slate Caverns,
Llanbedr, near Harlech
On tour 8, page 25

Portmeirion
On tour 8, page 25

Powis Castle, *Welshpool*
On tour 9, page 27

Rheidol Power Station, *Capel Bangor*
On tour 11, page 31

Rheidol Forest Visitor Centre
On tour 11, page 31

Strata Florida Abbey,
Pontrhydfendigaid
On tour 13, page 35

Talyllyn Railway and Museum,
Tywyn
On tour 10, page 29

Tom Norton's Cycle Collection,
Llandrindod Wells
On tour 12, page 33

Vale of Rheidol Railway,
Aberystwyth
On tour 11, page 31

Vyrnwy Visitor Centre
On tour 9, page 27

Welshpool and Llanfair Railway
On tour 9, page 27

South Wales

Within the boundaries of this great holiday region there's a wealth of unexpected contrasts – mountains and moorlands, forests and farmlands, market towns and modern cities, and a 300 mile long coastline of lively resorts and quieter villages. Just as varied are the holiday attractions, from caves to re-created coal mines, wildlife parks to giant pleasure parks.

Between the Pembrokeshire Coast National Park in the extreme west and the Wye Valley in the east there's a great diversity of landscapes. In the south-western corner are the broad bays and tiny inlets, long sandy beaches and rugged cliffs and headlands, best explored on foot along the Pembrokeshire Coast Path. Along this coast, you'll find some quiet coves as well as the more sophisticated resorts of Tenby and Saundersfoot, whose holiday attractions and facilities should satisfy the most fickle of visitors.

The Gower Peninsula, which makes a short circular tour in itself, has an equally impressive 'protected' coastline, designated an area of outstanding natural beauty. High cliffs and grassy headlands are interrupted only by a series of delightful sandy beaches. To the east of Swansea, between Aberavon and the well-known resort of Porthcawl, high dunes back an extensive beach. Beyond the Heritage Coast is the fun-packed Barry Island and Penarth.

To the north, lie the 519 square miles of the Brecon Beacons National Park, with its mountains that rise to over 2,900ft at the summit of Penyfan, its spectacular waterfalls, caves and forests.

Beyond the Black Mountain and the Beacons to the west is the Vale of Towy, with its quiet river scenery and lush farmlands, showing the gentler, almost pastoral face of the region. Similarly, the Vale of Glamorgan contrasts sharply with the steep-sided valleys of South Wales which cradled the Industrial Revolution. Many of these valleys are green again, providing all kinds of recreational facilities and

Top right: Barafundle Bay, on the Pembrokeshire Coast.

Opposite: Cardiff's city hall, part of the capital's stately civic centre.

Below: Tenby's colourful harbour.

unexpectedly beautiful mountain scenery. Bordering with England is the thickly wooded Wye Valley, the region's second area of outstanding natural beauty. Cardiff and Swansea, both recognised touring centres, have plenty of city-centre attractions too, including castles, museums, art galleries, theatres and cinemas.

Cardiff, the capital, is host to a number of major events, including the spectacular Searchlight Tattoo held within the grounds of Cardiff Castle, every two years. Not forgetting the many rugby events which have brought fame to the city and to Wales.

For more detailed information about South Wales, get your copy of the Wales Tourist Board's guide to the region, featured on the back of this book. A comprehensive gazetteer of towns and villages, and a useful beach guide are included. Available at leading booksellers, newsagents and information centres or direct from the *Wales Tourist Board, P.O. Box 1, Cardiff CF1 2XN.*

Places to visit in South Wales

The following attractions are on tour routes featured in this guide.

Abergavenny Castle and Museum
On tour 19, page 47

Afan Argoed Country Park and Miners' Museum
On tour 22, page 53

Barry Island Pleasure Park
On tour 24, page 55

Big Pit Mining Museum, *Blaenavon*
On tour 21, page 51

Brecon Beacons Mountain Centre
On tour 18, page 45

Brecon Cathedral
On tour 18, page 45

Brecon Mountain Railway, *Merthyr Tydfil*
On tour 18, page 45

Brecknock Museum, *Brecon*
On tour 18, page 45

Caerleon Roman Amphitheatre and Museum
On tour 20, page 49

Caerphilly Castle
On tour 21, page 51

Cardiff Castle
On city tour, page 56

Carmarthen Museum
On tour 17, page 43

Castell Carreg Cennen
On tour 17, page 43

Chepstow Castle
On tour 20, page 49

Craig-y-Nos Country Park, *Abercraf*
On tour 18, page 45

Cwmcarn Scenic Forest Drive
On tour 21, page 51

Dan-yr-Ogof Showcaves, *Abercraf*
On tour 18, page 45

Dolau Cothi Roman Gold Mines
On tour 17, page 43

Haverfordwest Castle and Museum
On tour 16, page 41

Lamphey Palace
On tour 16, page 41

Llandaff Cathedral
On city tour, page 56

Llandegfedd Reservoir
On tour 21, page 51

Llanthony Abbey
On tour 19, page 47

Manor House Wildlife and Leisure Park, *near Tenby*
On tour 16, page 41

Manorbier Castle
On tour 16, page 41

Margam Country Park
On tour 22, page 53

Monmouth Museum
On tour 20, page 49

Museum of the Woollen Industry, *Drefach Felindre*
On tour 14, page 37

National Museum of Wales, *Cardiff*
On city tour, page 56

Newport Museum and Art Gallery
On tour 21, page 51

Pembroke Castle
On tour 16, page 41

Penhow Castle
On tour 20, page 49

Penscynor Wildlife Park, *near Neath*
On tour 22, page 53

Picton Castle's Graham Sutherland Gallery
On tour 16, page 41

Raglan Castle
On tour 20, page 49

Richard Booth Secondhand Bookshop, *Hay on Wye*
On tour 19, page 47

St. David's Cathedral
On tour 15, page 39

Skenfrith and Grosmont Castles
On tour 19, page 47

Swansea Leisure Centre
On tour 23, page 54

Talley Abbey, *near Llandeilo*
On tour 17, page 43

Tenby Museum
On tour 16, page 41

Tintern Abbey
On tour 20, page 49

Tredegar House and Country Park, *Newport*
On tour 21, page 51

Tretower Court and Castle
On tour 19, page 47

Tudor Merchant's House, *Tenby*
On tour 16, page 41

Welsh Folk Museum, *St. Fagan's*
On city tour, page 56

Welsh Industrial and Maritime Museum, *Cardiff*
On city tour, page 56

Wolvesnewton Model Farm Folk Collection and Craft Centre, *near Usk*
On tour 20, page 49

Touring Tips

This book is intended as a family holiday guide, giving useful suggestions for things to see and do during your stay in Wales. With the increasing price of petrol, holiday travelling has to be purposeful. Gone are the days when you could drive off aimlessly hoping to find something of interest en route. With the aid of our easy-to-follow maps you will find plenty of fascinating things to see and do within a day's drive of your holiday base.

At the back of this book we have included a series of more detailed road maps covering the whole of Wales. If you feel you still need a separate road map, get a copy of the Wales Tourist Map, available at information centres, booksellers and newsagents.

The Maps

Each tour map shows the actual route, with road numbers, where applicable. Main towns and villages are shown, as well as tourist attractions and natural features, such as waterfalls and lakes. A series of symbols are used to denote most of the tourist attractions. The majority are self-explanatory, but if you're unsure please refer to the key opposite. A key map in the top left hand corners shows the tour in relation to the whole of Wales. Numbers in yellow refer to the route directions. Opposite each tour map is a brief description of some of the attractions worth visiting on or just off the route.

Touring Base

Each tour starts at a well known touring base, where there is usually an abundance of holiday accommodation. It is possible, too, to follow the tours from **any** point along the route specified. By referring to the appropriate detailed road map at the back of the book (see page references in top left hand corner) you could also join the route from any point within reasonable driving distance of the tour.

Key to Symbols

- ♜ *Castle*
- ♟ *Historic House*
- ▣ *Museum/Art Gallery*
- ♨ *Pottery*
- ℤ *Tourist Information Centre*
- AA RAC *A.A./R.A.C. Service Area*
- ✝ *Cathedral, abbey, priory or notable religious site*
- ⚲ *Roman Site*
- ⚭ *Prehistoric site of importance*
- ♇ *Early Christian Monument*
- ❀ *Nature Trail, Forest Trail, Town Trail and Heritage Trail.*
- ✗ *Craft Workshops*
- ⛟ *Narrow Gauge Railway*
- ⚘ *Woollen Mill*
- ⋔ *Country Park*
- ⋎ *Wildlife Park*
- ⚶ *Theatre*
- ⛏ *Caves open to Public*
- ⛏ *Site of Industrial Archaeological interest*
- ❊ *Garden*

Route Directions

The route is divided into a number of sections, with each stopping-off place or attraction of interest indicated by a number, which is keyed in to the tour map.

Abbreviations used: rt–*right*. m – *miles*. l – *left*. rb – *round-about*. S/P – *signposted*. N.T. – *National Trust*. E.C. – *Early Closing*. M.D. – *Market Day*. T.I.C. – *Tourist Information Centre*. E – *Easter to September*. C – *Charge* F – *Free*.

Mountain Roads

Wherever possible we have tried to include spectacular mountain roads and passes in the tours featured in this guide. Some of the finest passes are first class 'A' roads; for example the rugged Nant Ffrancon Pass, on the A5 south of Bethesda or Bwlch yr Oerddrws, near Dinas Mawddwy, on the A470-north-south trunk road. The most famous of all, the Llanberis Pass, is designated a clearway.

Also included in this guide is a number of 'off the beaten track' mountain routes along unclassified roads, which are steep, narrow in parts, with passing places. Those with a fear of dizzy heights would be wise to stick to the main classified roads.

Bwlch-y-Groes, the mountain pass from Dinas Mawddwy to Bala

Opening Times

Due to the fluctuation of times and prices, detailed information of this nature cannot be included in this guide. Under each attraction entry a general indication of the periods of opening is given. National Trust properties in Wales are generally open Easter to October, while all castles and historic places in the care of the Welsh Office are open all year. An asterisk * denotes those which are open during the following Standard Hours.

Always check opening times, wherever possible, if making a special journey to a specific site.

Months	Weekdays	Sundays
16 October- 14 March	9.30 a.m.- 4.00 p.m.	2.00 p.m.- 4.00 p.m.
15 March – 15 October	9.30 a.m.- 6.30 p.m.	2.00 p.m.- 6.30 p.m.

SM denotes those which are also open on Sun. mornings, April to September.

Dragon Routes

Look out for the specially signposted Dragon Holiday Routes when driving through Wales at peak summer weekends. When these signs are uncovered, it is usually advantageous to follow them, avoiding traffic congestion. *These routes are not suitable for caravans.*

Bed Booking Service

Most of the tourist information centres in Wales operate a Bed Booking Service, which is invaluable to touring visitors. Free of charge (a returnable deposit system), staff will arrange accommodation of all types and prices, in the locality or further afield. They could even make reservations for you along the routes featured in this guide.

Tolls

Tolls are payable on the following bridges and causeways:
● Severn Bridge (M4 motorway).
● Cleddau Bridge over Milford Haven.
● Porthmadog Causeway on A487 on east side of town.
● Penrhyndeudraeth – unclassified road between A496 and A487, 3½m east of Porthmadog towards Harlech.

Tourist Information Centres

When travelling around Wales look out for the 'i' sign which signifies a T.I.C. Over 70 centres are located at key points throughout the country to help you get the most out of your holiday. (Most of the touring bases in this guide have an information centre). Staff will handle enquiries on both a local and country-wide basis, suggesting places to visit and things to do. They can also provide you with detailed opening hours for many of the attractions featured in this guide.

Most of our Tourist Information Centres are open from Easter to mid September. *The following are, however, open all year.*

Aberystwyth T.I.C., *Eastgate, Aberystwyth, Dyfed. Tel. (0970) 612125.*
Cardiff T.I.C., *3 Castle Street, Cardiff. Tel. (0222) 27281.*
Colwyn Bay T.I.C., *Prince of Wales Theatre, Colwyn Bay, Clwyd. Tel. (0492) 30478.*
Llanberis T.I.C., *CEGB Centre, Llanberis, Gwynedd. Tel. (0286) 870765.*

Llandrindod Wells T.I.C., *Rock Park Spa, Llandrindod Wells, Powys. Tel. (0597) 4307.*
Machynlleth T.I.C., *Canolfan Owain Glyndwr, Machynlleth, Powys. Tel. (0654) 2401*
Menai Bridge T.I.C., *Coed Cyrnol, Menai Bridge, Isle of Anglesey, Gwynedd. Tel. (0248) 712626.*
Monmouth T.I.C., *Church Street, Monmouth, Gwent. Tel. (0600) 3899.*
Newport T.I.C., *Museum and Art Gallery, John Frost Square, Newport, Gwent. Tel. (0633) 842962.*
Newtown T.I.C., *Town Council Buildings, The Cross, Newtown, Powys. Tel. (0686) 25580.*
Ruthin T.I.C., *Craft Centre, Ruthin, Clwyd. Tel. (08242) 3992.*
Swansea Civic Information Centre, *P.O. Box 59, Singleton Street, Swansea SA1 3QG. Tel. (0792) 468321.*
Swansea T.I.C., *Ty Croeso, Gloucester Place, Swansea S4 1TY. Tel. (0792) 465204.*
Welshpool T.I.C., *Vicarage Garden Car Park, Welshpool, Powys. Tel. (0938) 2043.*

Do call in at one of the Wales Tourist Board's information centres when travelling around Wales.

TOUR 1
Isle of Anglesey

Base: *Menai Bridge*

See also page 61

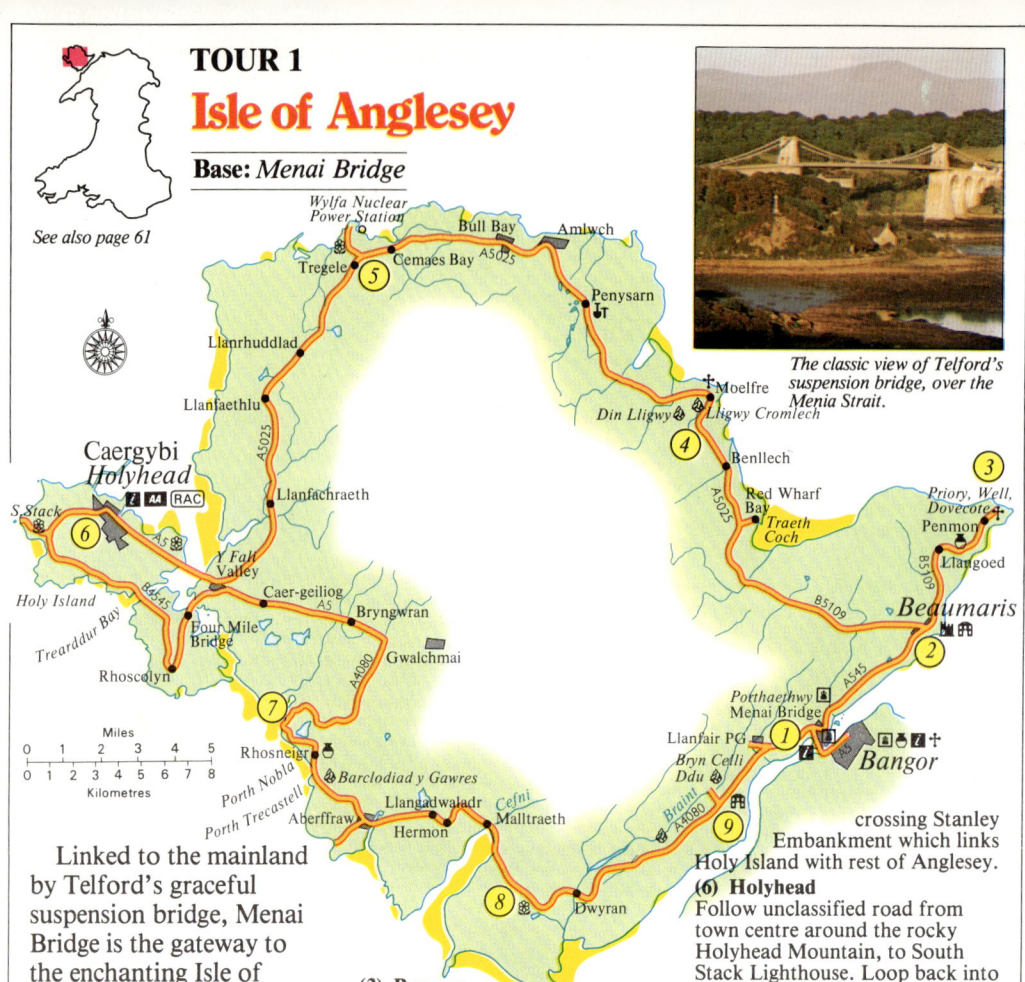

The classic view of Telford's suspension bridge, over the Menia Strait.

Linked to the mainland by Telford's graceful suspension bridge, Menai Bridge is the gateway to the enchanting Isle of Anglesey. Places of interest within the town include the Tegfryn Art Gallery, the nostalgic Museum of Childhood and the tiny church of St. Tysilio's, on an island in the Strait. *T.I.C. Isle of Anglesey Tourist Association, Coed Cyrnol.* Tel. Menai Bridge (0248) 712626 (1 – 12).

(1) START: Menai Bridge
Leave the town on A545, driving alongside the Strait to Beaumaris.

(2) Beaumaris
From this renowned sailing centre an unclassified road to Llangoed leads to the priory at Penmon in Anglesey's north-eastern corner.

(3) Penmon
Return on same route to Beaumaris and turn rt on B5109 for Pentraeth. At junction with A5025 turn rt, detouring if you wish to Red Wharf Bay. Continue on A5025, to roundabout S/P Moelfre.

(4) Moelfre
Take road to the rt for Moelfre. Detour on unclassified road to Din Lligwy (see opp) or return on to A5025, which rings the northern part of the island. Roads to rt lead to little beaches and bays including Amlwch and Bull Bay.

(5) Cemaes Bay to Valley
From rb on A5025 at Cemaes Bay, keep ahead for approx. 1m, turning rt for Wylfa Nuclear Power Station. Return to A5025 following the road around the quieter western side of the island to junction with A5 at Valley. At traffic lights turn rt on to A5, crossing Stanley Embankment which links Holy Island with rest of Anglesey.

(6) Holyhead
Follow unclassified road from town centre around the rocky Holyhead Mountain, to South Stack Lighthouse. Loop back into town, and follow road to rt to B4545 (detour to Rhoscolyn). Pass through Trearddur Bay, over Four Mile Bridge back to Valley, turning rt on to A5. In approx. 6m turn rt on to A4080 for Rhosneigr.

(7) Rhosneigr
From this little resort, follow A4080 around to the rt for Porth Trecastell, Aberffraw, Malltraeth.

(8) Newborough
Cross the Malltraeth Sands into Newborough where an unclassified road to rt takes you through the forest to miles of sandy beach. Return to A4080, turning rt for drive to Llanfairpwll.

(9) Plas Newydd
As the road runs parallel with the Strait, turn rt for visit to Plas Newydd, then return to Menai Bridge.

10

What to see

Museum of Childhood
Menai Bridge

Take a nostalgic step back in time to the days of your childhood at this gem of a museum in Water Street, off Uxbridge Square.

Exhibits include a super collection of dolls, clockwork toys, trains, music boxes, savings boxes and commemorative in glass and pottery, all depicting children's interests throughout the ages. A great place to take the children if the weather's a little unfavourable.
Tel. Menai Bridge (0248) 712498.
Open: Easter to October.
Car parks nearby.   **C.**

Tegfryn Art Gallery
Menai Bridge

Works by prominent contemporary Welsh artists are exhibited at this well-established private gallery, not far from the shore of the Menai Strait. Pictures may be purchased.
Tel. Menai Bridge (0248) 712437.
Open: Daily 10 am-5 pm. Closed lunchtimes. Closed Mon. October to Easter.
Car parks nearby.   **F.**

Beaumaris Castle

Beaumaris was the last link in Edward I's great network of castles in North Wales. Work began in 1295 and in three years this perfectly designed concentric

castle was defensible. The water-filled moat has been partially restored.
Open: All year. Standard Hours*
Also S.M. Free car park.   **C.**

Beaumaris Gaol

Prison life in Victorian times is vividly depicted in this gaol, which has remained virtually unaltered since it was built in 1829. The prison cells, a unique tread wheel and the condemned man's walk to the scaffold all serve as grim reminders of those harsh times.
Open: June to September only.   **C.**

Penmon Priory

A mediaeval monastery on the remote south-eastern tip of Anglesey, overlooking Ynys Seiriol, also known as Puffin Island. St. Seiriol's Well, nearby, is of 6th century origin, while the dovecote dates from about 1600.
Open: At any reasonable time.
Car park nearby.   **F.**

Din Lligwy Fortified Village
near Llanallgo.

Just off the tour route, at the Moelfre roundabout, an unclassified road leads to the remains of the native village of Din Lligwy, which dates from the 4th century. Walls of some of the stone huts stand to a height of 6ft. The Lligwy Burial Chamber close by has a massive capstone of 28 tons, measuring 18ft long by 15ft wide.
Open: At any reasonable time.   **F.**

Wylfa Nuclear Power Station

This station is located on Anglesey's rugged north coast. Tours of the power station are available from the Information Centre. The local headland was dedicated to the public by the CEGB and provides a walking area of scenic beauty and picinic site. An observation tower on the headland contains an exhibition about nuclear power.
Tel: Cemas Bay (0407) 710471
Please telephone for admission details.

South Stack Lighthouse

409 steps descent 350ft down to South Stack Lighthouse on Anglesey's north-west coast, Follow this short guided walk for views of sea bird colonies (May to mid July) and flowers of the coast. 3m west of Holyhead.

South Stack Lighthouse, near Holyhead

Plas Newydd (N.T.)
Near Llanfair P.G.

Plas Newydd, with its 169 acres of gardens and woodlands, bordering the Menai Strait, was first opened to visitors in 1969. One of the most outstanding rooms in this 18th century house, designed by James Wyatt Warren, is the

Rex Whistler Room, which has an impressive mural by the artist of the same name. This is considered to be the finest wall painting ever carried our in any country house in Britain. A Military Museum is housed in the Cavalry Room, devoted to the campaign relics (including uniforms and headdress) of the 1st Marquess of Anglesey who commanded the cavalry at Waterloo.
Open: Easter to October.
Free car park.   **C.**

Llanfairpwll Tourist Centre

The longest platform ticket in the world, bearing the town's 58 letter place name in full, is available at the B.R. Station. At the nearby Tourist Centre learn a little more about the Isle of Anglesey, its history and geology. A slide show featuring places of interest in the locality is an added attraction here.
Open: Station – all year.
Visitor Centre: Times to be confirmed.   **C.**

TOUR 2

Lleyn Peninsula

Base: *Caernarfon*

See also page 61

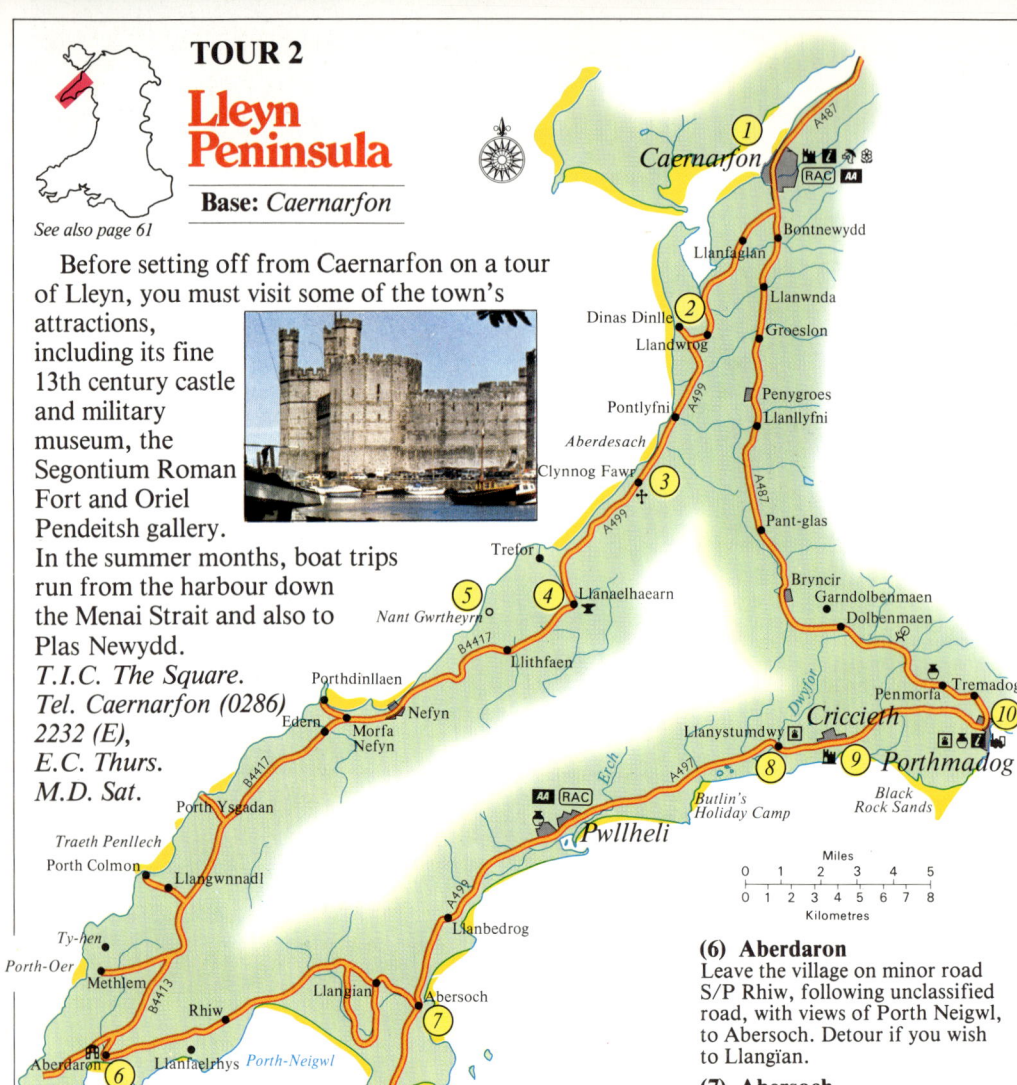

Before setting off from Caernarfon on a tour of Lleyn, you must visit some of the town's attractions, including its fine 13th century castle and military museum, the Segontium Roman Fort and Oriel Pendeitsh gallery.

In the summer months, boat trips run from the harbour down the Menai Strait and also to Plas Newydd.

T.I.C. The Square.
Tel. Caernarfon (0286) 2232 (E),
E.C. Thurs.
M.D. Sat.

(1) START: Caernarfon
From town centre, take A487 S/P Pwllheli. In approx. 1m turn rt S/P Llanfaglan and immediate rt. Follow Aber foreshore road for 4m. At Llandwrog turn rt for Dinas Dinlle, and rt again in ½m at T Junction, to beach.

(2) Dinas Dinlle
Road runs beside open stretch of seashore and beach. Return on tour route to A499. S/P Pwllheli.

(3) Clynnog
In 4m arrive at Clynnog for visit to 6th century church, or continue on A499, for approx. 4m.

(4) Llanaelhaearn
Here, take the rt fork off A499 on to B4417 S/P Nefyn and follow this road to Llithfaen. From crossroads detour to rt along narrow country road for Nant Gwrtheyrn (see opp).

(5) Nant Gwrtheyrn
From village, return to Llithfaen, and follow B4417 to Nefyn. Turn rt on square for Morfa Nefyn (1½m) or continue on B4417 and B4413 to Aberdaron.

(6) Aberdaron
Leave the village on minor road S/P Rhiw, following unclassified road, with views of Porth Neigwl, to Abersoch. Detour if you wish to Llangïan.

(7) Abersoch
From this yachting centre, detour to Trwyn Cilan for views of coast or follow A499 to Pwllheli. From town square, take A497, S/P Criccieth.

(8) Llanystumdwy
Visit Lloyd George Museum and riverside grave (limited parking), then drive on to Criccieth.

(9) Criccieth
Turn rt at village green for promenade and car park. Return on to A497 for drive to Porthmadog.

(10) Porthmadog
From main rb in the town, follow A487 via Tremadog, back to Caernarfon.

What to see

Caernarfon Castle

Probably the most famous of all the Welsh castles, built by Edward I as part of his great chain of fortresses. It has also earned its place in modern history, as the setting for the Investiture of H.R.H. Prince Charles as Prince of Wales in 1969. Within the castle there's a military museum of the Royal Welch Fusiliers plus film show on Caernarfon.
Open: All year. Standard Hours*. Also S.M. Car park – charge. **C.**

Segontium Roman Fort and Museum

Caernarfon

A branch of the National Museum of Wales displaying relics found on excavations at the Roman fort of Segontium, probably founded in 78 A.D.
Open: All year. Standard Hours*. **C.**

Criccieth's medieval castle.
Try your hand behind the potter's wheel at Porthmadog.

Nant Gwrtheyrn

Just off the Saints' route to Bardsey is Nant Gwrtheyrn, often described as a 'ghost village'. Once a thriving quarrying village it is now deserted and only accessible, from the car park above, down a steep and stony track. Its superb, isolated location has made it the obvious choice for Wales's first Welsh language centre.

Lloyd George Memorial Museum

Llanystumdwy

One of the most famous of Welshmen, Lloyd George, spent his childhood in the village of Llanystumdwy. His grave, on the banks of the River Dwyfor, is only a short walk from the Memorial Museum.
Open: end of May to end of September. 10am – 5pm, weekdays only. Limited parking. **C.**

Criccieth Castle

Crowning a rocky peninsula above the little seaside town of Criccieth are the remains of a native Welsh castle, later strengthened by Edward I. Strategically placed, it commands views of the bay.
Open: All year. Standard Hours*. Also S.M. **C.**

The Ffestiniog Railway

Porthmadog

Still popular as ever, the narrow gauge Ffestiniog Railway trundles its way through beautifully wooded countryside from the harbourside station at Porthmadog all the way to the fascinating slate town of

Blaenau Ffestiniog (where it connects with British Rail's scenic Conwy Valley line). A small museum is also located at Porthmadog Station.
Tel. Porthmadog (0766) 2384. Open: Late March to early Nov. Weekends only Feb. – March. Timetable on request. **C.**

Porthmadog Maritime Museum

In the Porthmadog Maritime Museum, housed in the cargo hold of a sailing ketch berthed in the harbour, displays illustrate harbour life here over 100 years ago, when slate was shipped all over the world. An authentic slate quay has also been recreated at No. 3 wharf, to complete the picture.
Open: Daily Easter to September. **C.**

Porthmadog Pottery

Here, in a former flour mill, you can watch all the processes in the manufacture of Porthmadog Pottery's colourful earthenware. You can even try your hand on the potter's wheel! In Snowdon Street.
Tel. Porthmadog (0766) 2785. Open: April to October, Mon-Fri. (daily July and August). **C.**

Brynkir Woollen Mill

Golan

A short detour off the main route (A487), 3m north of Porthmadog, for the village of Golan, will bring you to the Brynkir Woollen Mill. This is a small family-run mill in a lovely rural setting, producing traditional tapestries and tweeds.
Tel. Garndolbenmaen (076 675) 236 Open: All year. **F.**

TOUR 3
Snowdon

Base: *Betws-y-Coed*

See also page 61-2

The Swallow Falls at Betws-y-Coed

Popular Betws-y-Coed, surrounded on all sides by the Gwydyr Forest is well served by hotels and guest houses, as well as farm-houses and camp sites. Holiday activities here include walking the many forest trails, fishing for salmon on the Lledr, Llugwy and Conwy rivers, and, of course, touring Snowdonia. For such a small village there are plenty of things to see too – a Railway Museum, pottery, art gallery, a summer theatre for entertainment, and 2m. west, the famous Swallow Falls.

T.I.C. Tel. Betws-y-Coed (06902) 426 (E).

(1) START: Betws-y-Coed
From the centre of the village follow A5 over the Waterloo Bridge, past T.I.C. and take the first road to rt (A470) S/P to Dolgellau. Drive through the wooded Lledr Valley for

approx. 5m. to Dolwyddelan. Beyond the castle, the road climbs over the steep Crimea Pass (1263ft) down into Blaenau Ffestiniog.

(2) Blaenau Ffestiniog
Visit one of the two major slate attractions on the northern approach to the town (see opp). Then detour, if you wish, from town centre on B4414 to the Ffestiniog Power Station at Tanygrisiau. Otherwise continue on A470 for 1½m, bearing rt on to A496 for Maentwrog.

(3) Maentwrog
Joining A487 to rt at Maentwrog, turn rt by Oakley Arms for the winding road (B4410) through Rhyd to A4085. Turn rt here at T junction for the Aberglaslyn Pass and Beddgelert.

(4) Beddgelert
From Beddgelert's bridge, turn l. on to A4085 for Caernarfon, passing on your l. in 1½m the entrance to Beddgelert Forest.

(5) Rhyd Ddu
On entering Rhyd Ddu, in approx. 5m, note car park on rt – starting point for footpath to Snowdon. Drws-y-Coed Pass is to l. Llyn Cwellyn is on l. as you continue on A4085 to Caernarfon.

(6) Caernarfon
From main square, drive down to Slate Quay Car Park for visit to castle. From the same square, continue tour, taking road to rt, branching l. on to A4086 for Llanberis.

(7) Llanberis
In approx. 7m arrive in the village at the foot of Snowdon. Park by lakeside. Take your choice from the attractions featured opposite, then continue over the Llanberis Pass to Pen-y-Gwryd. Turn l. here, S/P Capel Curig.

(8) Capel Curig
At junction with A5 in Capel Curig turn rt for return to Betws-y-Coed.

What to see

Conwy Valley Railway Museum

Betws-y-Coed
See description on page 17.

Dolwyddelan Castle

Looking out over the rugged grandeur of Moel Siabod is the lonely castle of Dolwyddelan, reputedly the birthplace of Llywelyn the Great.
Open: All year. Any reasonable time.
Free car park.   **C.**

Caernarfon Castle
See description on page 13.

Segontium Roman Fort/Museum
See description on page 13.

Snowdon Mountain Railway

Llanberis
Opened in 1896 and operated entirely by coal fired steam locomotives, the railway climbs more than 3,000 ft to the Summit of Snowdon. On a fine day the views from the train are unsurpassed. The round trip from Llanberis to the Summit and back lasts 2½ hours including a ½ hour stay at the Summit. Cafe and shops at Llanberis and Summit Stations. **N.B.** Intending passengers are advised to telephone General Manager's Office for details of trains on day of proposed visit as demand is heavy in high season. Weather on Snowdon is notoriously unpredictable.
Tel. Llanberis (0286) 870223
Open: Week before Easter to early October. Adequate parking.   **C.**
From Llanberis the mountain railway runs to the summit of Snowdon.

Llanberis Lake Railway

A 2 mile section of the Llanberis Lake Railway, originally built to carry slates to Port Dinorwic on the Menai Strait. The scenic narrow-gauge line has two stopping places from which passengers can explore the lake shore.
Tel. Llanberis (0286) 870549
Open: Easter to late September. Limited service in spring and autumn. Free car park.   **C.**

The Welsh Slate Museum

Llanberis
The great days of the slate industry are again recalled at this

"Ladies" and "Duchesses" have a completely new meaning for former slate quarrymen.

museum in the former workshops of the Dinorwic Quarry, in the Padarn Country Park. Much of the original machinery remains intact in the quarry workshops, including a giant waterwheel, over 50ft in diameter. There is also a working smithy. In a special cinema/gallery, films about the industry are shown at regular intervals.
Tel. Llanberis (0286) 870630
Open: Easter to September daily. Free car park.   **C.**

Llechwedd Slate Caverns

Blaenau Ffestiniog
Visitors have the choice of two exciting rides underground into the heart of the Llechwedd Slate Caverns. A narrow gauge tramway runs through tunnels and massive caverns where Victorian slate mining conditions have been vividly recreated. To explore the spectacular lower depths of the

The new incline at the Llechwedd Slate Caverns, Blaenau Ffestiniog, is Britain's steepest underground passenger railway.

mine a specially designed incline railway runs down a very steep gradient to the lower floors. Here, by means of effective audio-visual techniques, visitors are told something of the social life of the men who created these mines. Back on the surface, in the Slate Heritage Theatre, a 25 minute programme illustrates the story of the slate industry from its early beginnings, while in the Mill, with its display of mining equipment, the Slate Splitter can be seen at work. Cafe and restaurant on site, as well as Craft Workshop and Shop.
Tel. Blaenau Ffestiniog (0766) 830306
DO wear warm clothing. Open: Easter to October. Free car park.   **C.**

Gloddfa Ganol Slate Mine

An open-air museum with a difference – 1000ft up in the hills of Blaenau Ffestiniog. Pick up your helmets and walk through part of the old slate mine or be more adventurous and take the special Land Rover Conducted Tours to explore some of the chambers and tunnels, hundreds of feet up in the mountain. Massive machinery of the slate era is housed in an operational mill, while in the Interpretation Museum, overlooking the workings, the story of slate is told by means of informative displays. And for all railway enthusiasts a Narrow Gauge Railway Centre has opened here, exhibiting an amazing collection of locomotives and rolling stock. Restaurant, cafe and craft shop.
Tel. Blaenau Ffestiniog (0766) 830664. Easter to October. Free car park.   **C.**

Conwy Valley

Base: *Llandudno*

See also page 61-2

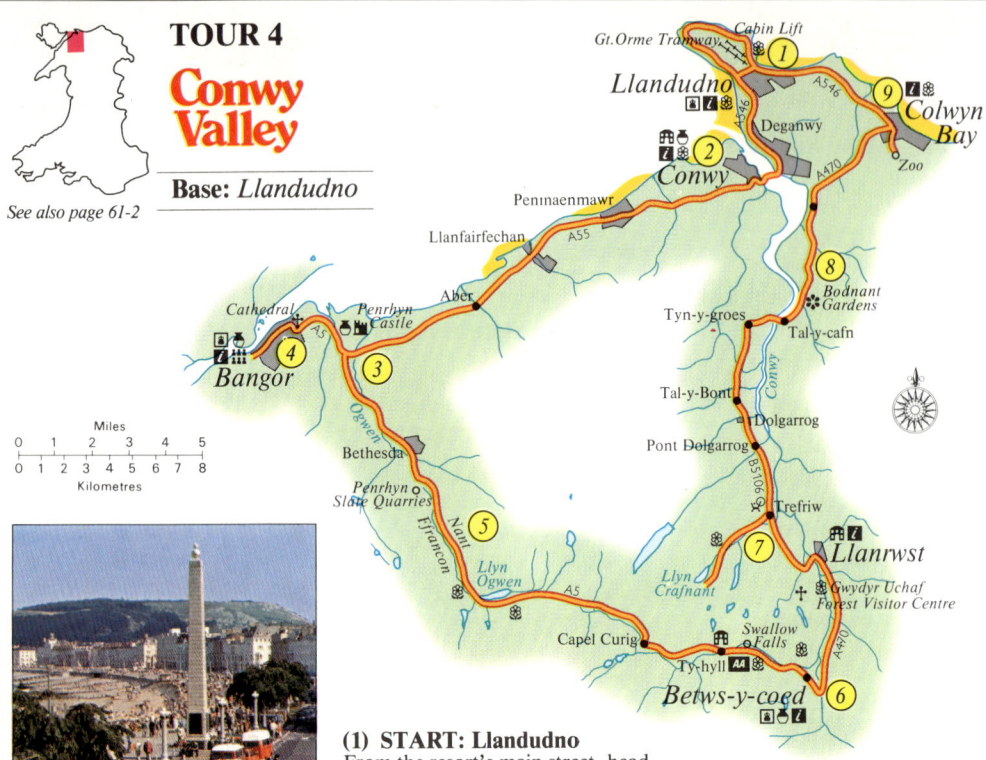

Miles
0 1 2 3 4 5
0 1 2 3 4 5 6 7 8
Kilometres

Llandudno, with its elegant hotel-lined Edwardian promenade, has plenty of holiday attractions: two superb beaches, a cabinlift and cable railway, gardens, golf courses, swimming pool and, in the summer months, a lively night-life with entertainment for all the family.

Only a short drive away are dozens more exciting places to visit, some of which are described opposite.

T.I.C. Chapel Street. Tel. (0492) 76413 (1 – 12). Also kiosks at Arcadia Theatre and North Promenade in summer.

(1) START: Llandudno
From the resort's main street, head for Conwy via Deganwy, crossing the road bridge which lies parallel with Telford's gracious suspension bridge.

(2) Conwy to Sychnant Pass
Following the A55 S/P Bangor by the castle walls, take a l. turn off the one-way system, S/P Sychnant Pass. This road, steep in parts, offers superb views as you descend back on to the A55 in Penmaenmawr in approx. 4m.

(3) Penmaenmawr to Penrhyn Castle
Continue along the A55 coast road, through the small resorts of Penmaenmawr and Llanfairfechan, to its junction with the A5 at Llandegai (Traffic Lights). On the rt is the main entrance for Penrhyn Castle (N.T.). Turn 1. for Nant Ffrancon Pass, on the A5, S/P Betws-y-Coed.

(4) Detour to Bangor
From Penrhyn Castle, take A5 for 2m detour into Bangor centre.

(5) Bangor to Nant Ffrancon
Return to A5/A55 junction, turning rt for continuation of tour to Nant Ffrancon Pass, stopping for views of Tryfan's 3,010ft peak and the Ogwen Lake and Falls.

(6) Nant Ffrancon to Betws-y-Coed
The fast, but scenic, A5, now takes you through the mountain village of Capel Curig into the famous inland resort of Betws-y-Coed.

(7) Trefriw and detour to Llyn Crafnant
From the wooded setting of Betws-y-Coed, cross the Waterloo Bridge (beyond Information Centre) taking immediately l. turn onto A470. S/P Conwy. In approx. 3m in Llanrwst, turn l. for B5106 to Trefriw. (Detour can be made to Llyn Crafnant for picnic, also Gwydyr Castle and Forest Visitor Centre.)

(8) Trefriw to Bodnant Garden
From village centre, continue n. on B5106 to Tynygroes turning rt for Talycafn on A470. Bodnant Garden (N.T.) is on l., approx. 2½m in direction of Llandudno. You can also visit the nearby Felin Isaf Flour Mill at Glan Conwy.

(9) Colwyn Bay
For detour to Colwyn Bay and Mountain Zoo, turn rt at major rb in further 2m. Otherwise return to Llandudno via Deganwy (A470) or Rhos on Sea (A546).

What to see

Llandudno Cabinlift and Tramway

Llandudno's 679ft high Great Orme summit can be reached from the Happy Valley by an exciting ride on the longest cable car system in Britain. The Great Orme Tramway, which has been carrying passengers to the summit since 1902, provides an alternative means of ascent.
Tramway − Tel. Llandudno (0492) 79749; Cabinlift − Tel. 77205. Both open Easter to October. **C.**

Llandudno Doll Museum and Model Railway

As well as a valuable collection of dolls from all over the world, the museum has one room set aside for a working model railway and a display of tinplate engines. In Masonic Street, opposite the Palladium.
Tel. Llandudno (0492) 76312. Open: Easter to September. **C.**

Conwy Castle

Possibly the most famous of Edward I's network of fortresses in North Wales. The massive town walls are equally impressive, overlooking the busy quayside and town centre.
Open: Standard Hours*. Also S.M. **C.**

Aberconwy House (N.T.)

Conwy

Apart from its magnificent castle, Conwy has a number of small, but architecturally interesting buildings. Aberconwy House is one of the last remaining mediaeval timber framed buildings in the town. An informative 'History of Conwy' exhibition illustrates the life of the borough from Roman times to the present day.
Open: Easter to October. **C.**

Conwy Valley Railway Museum

Betws-y-Coed

Standard gauge rolling stock and other items reflecting the various aspects of railway life are exhibited at this museum, situated in the old Goods Yard of Betsw-y-Coed B.R. Station. Light refreshment available.
Tel: Betws-y-Coed (06902) 568. Open: Easter to October. **C.**

Trefriw Woollen Mills

All the processes in the manufacture of raw wool to tailored garment − carding, spinning, dyeing, weaving etc. − on display. In the heart of the village. Mill Shop.
Tel: Llanrwst (0492) 640462. Open: Mon to Fri, 9am-5.30pm all year (check hours in winter) **F.** *(except school parties)*

Bodnant Garden

Considered to be one of the finest gardens in Britain, Bodnant has a magnificent collection of rhododendrons, camellias, magnolias and conifers. Main entrance ½m along Eglwysbach road, off A470.
Open: Mid March to end of October. Free car park. **C.**

Welsh Mountain Zoo

Colwyn Bay

A unique Mountain Zoo and firm family favourite. Children will love the daily sea lion display and falconry demonstration, their own 'children's zoo' and the galaxy of animals, birds and reptiles in natural surroundings, overlooking the Bay. Restaurant provided.
Tel: Colwyn Bay (0492) 2938. Open: All year. 10am-dusk. Free car park. **C.**

Colwyn Bay's Mountain Zoo.

Plas Mawr

Conwy

Claimed to be the finest Elizabethan town house in Britain, Plas Mawr in Conwy's High Street now serves as headquarters for the Royal Cambrian Academy of Art. Regular exhibitions held all year.**C.**

Penrhyn Castle (N.T.)

More of a stately home than a castle, Penrhyn is a masterpiece of Neo-Norman design. The exterior − castellated and stark, with massive walls − is surrounded by well-kept lawns. Within the castle is a wealth of wood and stone carving. Penrhyn's appeal is also enhanced by its natural history collection, doll's museum and industrial locomotive museum.
Open: Easter to October Free car park. **C.**

Museum of Welsh Antiquities

Ffordd Gwynedd, Bangor

A museum of local history, illustrating Welsh rural crafts of the past, pre-historic and Romano-British antiquities, costumes, furniture, ceramics, maps and prints.

Bangor Art Gallery, housed in the same building, has monthly touring exhibitions of paintings and/or sculpture.
Tel. Bangor (0248) 51151. Open: All year. **F.**

Further holiday attractions
Indoor Swimming Pools: Bangor; Colwyn Bay; Llandudno; Llanrwst.
Theatres: Bangor (all yr); Llandudno; Colwyn Bay.
Potteries: Bangor; Betws-y-Coed; Conwy; Penrhyn Castle.
Galleries: Llandudno − Rapallo House; Oriel Mostyn.
Waterfalls: Betws-y-Coed; Nant Ffrancon.
Dinosaur World: Colwyn Bay.

TOUR 5
Vale of Clwyd

Base: *Rhyl*

See also page 62-3

One of North Wales's main seaside resorts, full of attractions and entertainment for all the family. Children will love the 3 miles of sandy beaches, the Ocean Beach Pleasure Park, sporting facilities and the amazing new Sun Centre and Leisure Complex. Good value-for-money accommodation, with a range of hotels, guest houses and holiday caravan parks. *T.I.C. Town Hall. Tel. (0745) 31515 (1 – 12).*

(1) START: Rhyl
From central promenade, drive ahead on A525 for approx. 3 m to rb on northern approach to Rhuddlan.

(2) Rhuddlan to St. Asaph
Follow A525 to the town centre for visit to castle, then continue on this same road to the cathedral city of St. Asaph and then to Denbigh.

(3) Denbigh
Turn rt into centre of this historic town. The tour then continues on same A525 through the lovely Vale of Clwyd to Ruthin.

(4) Ruthin
You can call in at the Ruthin Craft Centre in the town. From the main square, where mediaeval traditions are revived on summer Wednesdays, return on to A525 S/P Wrexham for continuation of tour.

(5) Bwlchgwyn to Erddig
Approaching Bwlchgwyn, visit Milestone Museum on rt, then keep on same route (A525). At first major rb take road to rt S/P Shrewsbury for 2m approx. Here at second rb, turn l. for Erddig.

(6) Wrexham
Now follow signs into town centre. Take A541 to Mold (11½m).

(7) Mold
At major rb, turn rt for Theatr Clwyd, or stay on A541 ahead for Rhydymwyn and Nannerch. Turn rt on to B5121 over to Holywell.

(8) Holywell
At junction with A55, turn l. then rt for town centre, and its attractions. Return to main junction, turn rt and follow A5 for approx. 3m, passing Grange Military Museum on l. Bear l. on to A5151 for return journey.

(9) Bodrhyddan Hall
Beyond Dyserth visit Bodrhyddan Hall, then continue on A5151 to Rhuddlan or take alternative B5119 back to Rhyl.

What to see

Rhuddlan Castle

Edward I strategically placed this castle beside the river Clwyd and on the main coast route into North Wales.
Open: All year. Standard Hours*. Also S.M. Free car park. **C.**

Denbigh Castle and Town Walls

Overlooking the town from Denbigh Hill is the castle, built between 1282 and 1333. Its most notable feature is the sturdy triangular gatehouse with its statue reputedly of Edward I. Within the castle, a museum illustrates the monuments and its famous explorer, Sir Henry Morton Stanley.
Open: All year. Standard Hours*. Castle also open S.M. Free car park. **C.**

Erddig (N.T.)

near Wrexham

Late 17th century house with 18th century additions, and containing much of the original furniture; garden restored to its 18th century formal design, containing varieties of fruit known to have been grown there during that period. The range of domestic out-buildings includes laundry, bakehouse, sawmill and smithy, all in working order; also Agricultural Museum with a collection of local farm machinery mainly from the

second half of the 19th century, some of which is housed in a 17th century demountable barn; exhibition depicting the changes on the Erddig estate.
Open: Easter to late October. **C.**

Milestone Museum

Bwlchgwyn

A geological museum showing the development of North Wales over 600 million years. Step back in time here in the Time Tunnel or follow the Geological Trail, in the adjacent silica quarry. Other exhibits include a dinosaur display – always popular with children – and a stone garden.
Tel. Wrexham (0978) 757573.
Open: Easter to October, otherwise by appointment. Free car park. **C.**

Theatr Clwyd

Mold

Part of the chain of purpose-built regional theatres established in Wales in recent years, providing a varied programme of family entertainment throughout the year. Additional facilities at Theatr Clwyd include a cinema, restaurant, bar and gallery, all designed to give visitors an enjoyable evening out at the theatre.
Tel: Mold (0352) 56331. Open: All year. Free car park. **C.**

St. Winifred's Well

Holywell

One of the traditional 'seven wonders of Wales' and a place of pilgrimage for centuries, this holy well is dedicated to a 7th century saint.
Open: St. Winifred's Chapel, Fri and Sat, April to Sept. **F.**

Basingwerk Abbey

Holywell

Ruins of a monastery founded in 1131 by the French Savignac order, in a partly rural setting in the once industrial Greenfield Valley. Accessible along footpath off A548, 1m nw of Holywell in village of Greenfield.
Open: At any reasonable time, March to September. **F.**

Holywell Textile Mills

Welsh flannel has been produced here at the mills since the 18th century. Today's visitors may watch wool spun and woven into blankets, traditional and more contemporary tweeds, Welsh flannels and furnishings. Guided tours by arrangement.
Tel. Holywell (0352) 712022.
Open: All year. Mill – Mon to Fri. Shop – Mon to Sat. Free car park. **F.**

The Grange Cavern Military Museum

near Holywell

This is the world's largest underground military museum. Over 70 military vehicles – including armoured cars, jeeps and artillery pieces – are housed in a 2½ acre floodlit cavern. Also a large collection of militaria and specialist military items. Free film show. Picnic area.
Tel. Holywell (0352) 713455. Open: All year. Summer 9am-6pm, Winter 10am-5pm. Free car park. **C.**

Bodrhyddan Hall

near Rhuddlan.

Sir John Conwy, ancestor of the present owner, Lord Langford, completed the major part of the hall in 1696. Amongst the treasured collection of armour are two suits believed to be relics of the Wars of the Roses. This stately home also has some notable paintings and furniture.
Tel: Rhuddlan (0745) 590400.
Open: Tues and Thurs afternoons, June to Sept. Free car park. **C.**

Lakelands & Moorlands

Base: *Bala*

See also pages
62, 64

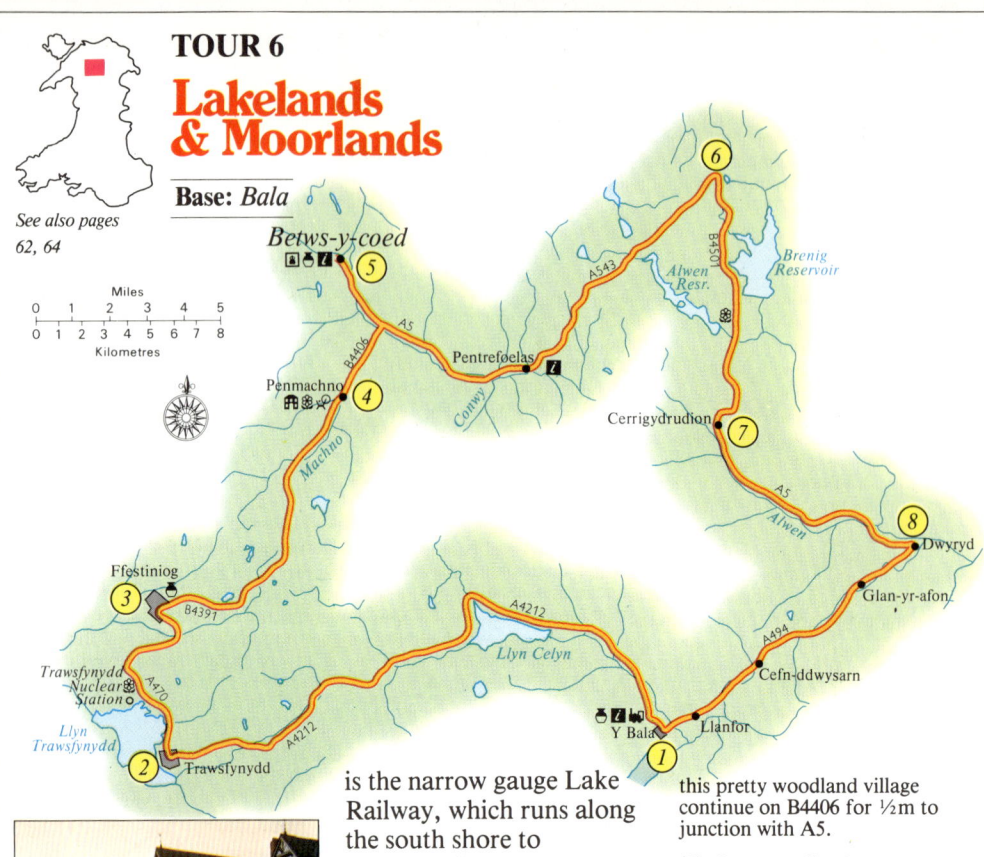

Miles
0 1 2 3 4 5
0 1 2 3 4 5 6 7 8
Kilometres

Located at the northern end of Llyn Tegid, Wales's largest natural lake, Bala has become in recent years an established inland sailing centre. Other holiday activities in the area include fishing, canoeing, golf, pony trekking and hill walking in the Aran, Arennig and Berwyn Mountains. A major attraction within the town

is the narrow gauge Lake Railway, which runs along the south shore to Llanuwchllyn.
T.I.C. Snowdonia National Park Visitor Centre, High Street. Tel. (0678) 520367(E). E.C. Wed.

(1) START: Bala
Our tour starts from Ffrydan Road, off High Street, following the scenic A4212 which runs alongside Llyn Celyn with views of the twin peaks of the Arennig mountains.

(2) Trawsfynydd
At junction with A470, turn rt, passing the nuclear power station and Trawsfynydd Lake.

(3) Ffestiniog
In less than 3m turn rt with the A470, S/P Betws-y-Coed. At Ffestiniog in a further 3m approx. turn rt on to B4391, then on the B4407 to the l. for the exciting drive over the Migneint Pass.

(4) Penmachno
From the woollen mill, perched on the edge of the Machno River, in

this pretty woodland village continue on B4406 for ½m to junction with A5.

(5) Betws-y-Coed
Turn l. on to A5 for detour to Betws-y-Coed (see page 14) or turn rt on main tour route.

(6) Pentrefoelas-Denbigh Moors
In 5m approx. at Pentrefoelas turn l. on to A543 on to the straight-as-a-die road over the Denbigh Moors. By the Sportsman's Arms turn rt on the new road to the Brenig Reservoir.

(7) Cerrigydrudion
From the Brenig Reservoir, return via B4501 to the A5 at Cerrigydrudion. Detour on to the B5105 for the Bod Petrual Visitor Centre in the Clocaenog Forest. To shorten the tour, 1m beyond Cerrigydrudion, turn rt on to B4501 for journey back to Bala.

(8) Detour to Ruthin
From the forestry centre, continue on B5105 to Ruthin (visiting the Ruthin Craft Centre), returning to Bala via A494. At Junction of A494 and A5, turn l. for detour to Corwen, or rt to traffic lights at Druid's Corner, turning l. for 9m drive to Bala.

What to see

Bala Lake Railway
See description on page 27.

Railway Museum
Betws-y-Coed
See description on page 17.

Penmachno Woollen Mill
A historic mill in a lovely woodland setting on the banks of the Machno river and waterfalls. In the 18th century it was a 'pandy' where cottage weavers brought their cloth to be washed and finished. Now a thriving mill weaving beautiful tweeds. An attractive craft shop sells the mill rugs and tweeds plus Wales's most fashionable collection of colour co-ordinated tweed clothes and knitwear. An audio-visual show 'The Story of Wool' is on site (small charge).

Open: March to October inclusive. Weaving Mon. to Fri. Wool Craft Shop: March to October, 7 days a week; but early and late season not open Sunday mornings.

Ty Mawr Wybrnant (N.T.)
Nr. Penmachno
This stone-built cottage, owned by the National Trust, is the birthplace of Bishop William Morgan (born 1541) who translated the Bible into Welsh. His translation, which is considered a literary masterpiece, became the foundation of modern Welsh literature. To get to the cottage, turn rt by Eagles Hotel, in Penmachno and follow road for about ½m, then bear rt.
Open: Daily, excl. Mon. and Sat. Easter to September. **C.**

Bod Petrual Visitor Centre
An exhibition presenting the Clocaenog Forest in its ecological and historical setting is the main feature of this visitor centre housed in a converted keeper's cottage in the forest. The centre is the start for a series of waymarked walks through woodlands of many species around the lakeside nearby, with glimpses of the moors beyond Facilities for disabled visitors. Picnic sites. Free car park.
Open: Centre − Easter to October. Walks − all year. **F.**

Brenig Centre
Located at the dam head of this huge new reservoir, the Centre introduces visitors to the history, environment and contemporary role of the surrounding Hiraethog moorlands, forest and man-made lake. Display and interpretive material cover topics as diverse as wildlife, dam construction, bygone times at the old farmsteads and present day recreation and leisure at Brenig.
Open: All year. 2pm − 5pm or dusk, Mon − Fri. 1pm − 7pm or dusk at weekends. **F.**

The exhibition centre at Llyn Brenig tells the story of the surrounding area.

Penmachno's delightfully-situated woollen mill.
Traditional Welsh weaves are produced inside the mill.

Berwyn Mountains

Base: *Llangollen*

See also pages 63, 65

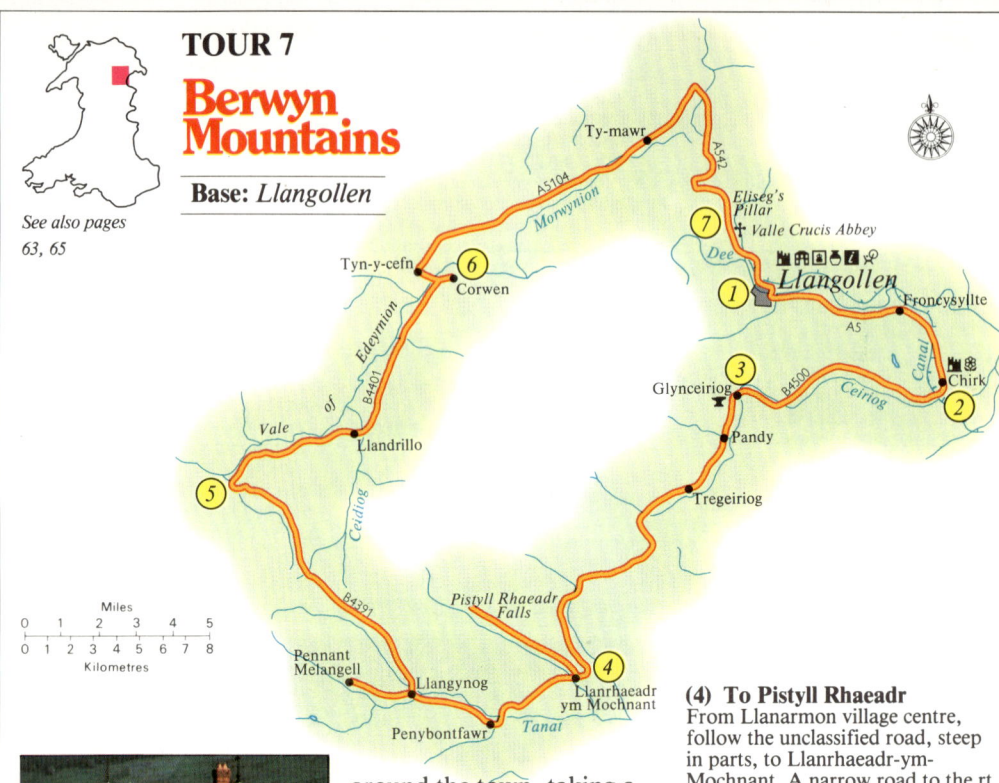

Though so close to the border, Llangollen is very much the typical Welsh market town. But what makes it so very unique is the annual International Musical Eisteddfod.

The town makes a perfect setting, tucked beneath the hills of the Clwydian mountains, in the wooded valley of the Dee. A day or even more can easily be spent wandering around the town, taking a walk along the towpath or cruising down the Llangollen Canal or climbing up to Castell Dinas Bran, a mediaeval castle 1,000 ft above the town.
T.I.C. Town Hall. Tel. (0978) 860828(E). E.C. Thurs. M.D. Tues.

(1) START: Llangollen
From town centre, turn l. at traffic lights on to A5, S/P Shrewsbury.

(2) Chirk
Approaching Chirk town centre, turn rt by Craft Shop for visit to castle (N.T.) or continue through main street for 100 yds, turning rt on sharp bend on to B4500 S/P Glyn Ceiriog. Follow this road into the lovely Ceiriog Valley.

(3) Glyn Ceiriog
From this well known pony trekking centre then continue through the valley on this 'B' road to the village of Llanarmon.

(4) To Pistyll Rhaeadr
From Llanarmon village centre, follow the unclassified road, steep in parts, to Llanrhaeadr-ym-Mochnant. A narrow road to the rt from the village square leads to the famous waterfall, known as Pistyll Rhaeadr. Return to village square, crossing bridge and driving uphill (2½m) to join B4391 at Penybontfawr.

(5) Penybontfawr to Corwen
Arriving at Penybontfawr, turn rt on B4391, for Llangynog. Continue on this 'B' road through Berwyn Mountains for 9m approx, turning rt by telephone kiosk on to B4402. In just over 1m turn rt to B4401 for Llandrillo and Cynwyd.

(6) Corwen and Llantysilio Mountain
At junction with main A5 road, turn rt for ½m detour into the market town of Corwen. Alternatively turn l., and in ½m at traffic lights, turn on to A494 S/P Ruthin. In 1m approx. take rt fork on to A5104 S/P Chester for approx 10m.

(7) Horseshoe Pass
At rb, take road to rt (A542) S/P Llangollen. This takes you over the Horseshoe Pass. Downhill on your l. is the Pillar of Eliseg and the gracious ruins of Valley Crucis Abbey (see opp). Follow this road back into Llangollen.

What to see

Chirk Castle (N.T.)

Enter Chirk Castle by the 18th century wrought iron gates, made by the Davies brothers of Bersham. Founded c.1310 as a strategic border fortress the elegant interior now incorporates the styles of various periods. Of interest: State Rooms, panelled Long Gallery, a collection of armour and other relics. The garden is of a formal nature with lawns surrounded by clipped yews.
Open: Easter to October. Free car park. **C.**

Plas Newydd
Llangollen

Originally the home of eccentrics, Lady Eleanor Butler and the Hon. Sarah Ponsonby, later to be known as the 'Ladies of Llangollen'. Here in this lovely black and white half-timbered mansion overlooking the Dee, they entertained many illustrious

Plas Newydd, in the lovely valley of the Dee, was the home of the Ladies of Llangollen.

visitors, including Byron, Shelley and Wordsworth. A small museum illustrates their days at Plas Newydd.
Open: May 1 – September. Free car park. **C.**

Llangollen Weavers
Dee Lane, Llangollen

Housed in a former corn mill on the banks of the Dee is this workshop where distinctive fabrics (tweeds and tapestry) are woven. Visitors can watch the weavers at work.
Open: All year. Daily, excluding winter Suns. Free car park.

Chwarel Wynne Mine and Museum
Glyn Ceiriog

Fascinating guided tours are given through this old slate mine, located on a beautiful, wooded 12 acre hillside site.
Tel. (069 172) 343
Open: Easter to end of September, 10 am – 5pm daily. Rest of year by appointment. **C.**

Valle Crucis Abbey

Coming down the Horseshoe Pass, on your l. hand side, are the serene ruins of the Cistercian Valle Crucis Abbey. Founded in 1201, it was built on simple lines in keeping with the Cistercians' usual lack of ostentation.
Open: Standard Hours*. Also S.M. Free car park. **C.**

Castell Dinas Bran
Llangollen

Overlooking the lovely Vale of Llangollen, is the superbly-sited Castell Dinas Bran. Cross the bridge over the Dee and the canal, and follow the signposted footpath to the hilltop remains of the castle, which was probably the impregnable stronghold for Gruffudd ap Madoc, one of the native Welsh princes.
Open: At any reasonable time. **F.**

Eliseg's Pillar

If you've travelled along the Horseshoe Pass before, you may well have wondered about the history relating to this 8ft high pillar, set on a mound, not far from the road. Its Latin inscription tells us it was erected in the 9th century by Prince Cyngen, in memory of his grandfather, Eliseg.
Open: At any reasonable time. **F.**

Pistyll Rhaeadr

From Llanrhaeadr, follow the lower of the two valley roads up to the Berwyns, and to Pistyll Rhaeadr. With a fall of 240ft this spectacular waterfall is reputed to be the highest in Wales. Only limited parking. To be avoided on peak holiday weekends.

Pistyll Rhaeadr, reputedly the highest waterfall in Wales.

Llangollen Canal Exhibition Centre

With the imaginative use of audio visual material, the story of the canals in Britain unfolds in a most entertaining way at this small, but fascinating museum, housed in an early 19th century warehouse. As well as showing, by means of working and static models, how the canals worked, this museum also gives an insight into the lives of those who built and worked on Britain's first major transport system.
Open: Easter; then Whitsun to end of September, daily. **C.**

TOUR 8

Cambrian Coast

Base: *Barmouth*

See also page 64

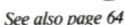

Barmouth, a small resort on the Cambrian Coast, offers the best of both worlds, being so conveniently placed for touring coast and country. Just on its doorstep are miles of wonderful walks along the Mawddach Estuary, generally recognised as one of Wales's most scenic locations, and in the hills of Snowdonia. Within the resort there's a good sandy beach, backed by a R.N.L.I. museum and a children's play area, and on the promenade in the summer months, an amusement park.
T.I.C. The Old Library. Tel. (0341) 280787(E). E.C. Wed.

(1) START: Barmouth
From the resort centre, take A496 northwards, S/P Harlech, driving through the villages of Talybont, Llanddwywe and Dyrffyn Ardudwy, with views of the coast to the l. and Snowdonia to the rt.

In approx. 9m arrive in Llanbedr. Detour to l. for Shell Island (S/P Mochras) and to rt. for Cwm Nantcol.

(2) Llanbedr to Llanfair
Remaining on tour route, continue along the A496 to Harlech, stopping off at Llanfair for visit to Old Quarries on rt (see opp.)

(3) Harlech via Maentwrog
The tour continues from Harlech, along A496 to Maentwrog, turning left at junction with A487. S/P Porthmadog. In 6m at Minffordd turn l. for Portmeirion (S/P). (Shorter alternative route: Approx. 1¾m beyond Talsarnau on A496, bear l. on to toll road to Penrhyndeudraeth, joining A487 to the l. for Minffordd).

(4) Portmeirion
Following visit to this Italianate village (see opp.) continue on A487, crossing the Cob (toll payable) into Porthmadog.

(5) Porthmadog to Tremadog
From town centre, stay on A487 for approx. 1½m to the town of Tremadog.

(6) Tremadog to Maentwrog
From the well-proportioned square at Tremadog, turn rt on to A498. In approx. 2½m beyond Glaslyn Inn, at Prenteg, turn rt on to B4410 to Garreg. Here at junction with A4085, drive straight across to Rhyd and Tanybwlch, joining A487 by Oakley Arms, Maentwrog.

(7) Maentwrog to Trawsfynydd
Continue on A487 and the fast A470 to Trawsfynydd. Note power station and lake on your rt.

(8) Ganllwyd
In a further 7m at the bridge over the River Eden, where road narrows, turn l. into forest picnic site and car park or rt to visitor centre. Otherwise continue via Ganllwydd to Lanelltyd. Detour over bridge to Cymer Abbey.

(9) Llanelltyd to Barmouth
The return journey along A496 takes you from Llanelltyd to Barmouth, overlooking the Mawddach Estuary for much of the way.

What to see

Harlech Castle

Mighty Harlech Castle stands on a rocky outcrop overlooking Tremadog Bay, with the Snowdonia range of mountains providing a suitably striking backdrop. Its main feature is a massive, almost impregnable gatehouse.
Open: All year. Standard Hours*. Also S.M. Car park nearby. **C.**

Portmeirion

near Penrhyndeudraeth

To many, this delightful Italianate village − created by architect Sir Clough Williams Ellis − will always be remembered as the dramatic setting for the popular T.V. series 'The Prisoner'. It is quite unique, scenically located on the shores of Traeth Bach, with the mountains of Snowdonia rising in the distance.

The architectural fantasy also contains shops, self-service restaurant, acres of woodlands and unspoilt sandy beaches. All the cottages in the village are let as holiday accommodation. Hotel at present under reconstruction.
Tel: Penrhyndendraeth (0766) 770228. Open: Daily Easter to October. Free car park. **C.**

Old Llanfair Quarry Slate Caverns

near Harlech

Chwarel Hen, just off the A496 at Llanfair, is a small slate mine, which visitors may explore, led by knowledgeable guides who explain the methods of mining in the last century. Authentic quarrymen's safety helmets provided. Underground temperature in the tunnels and caverns rarely exceeds 50°F, so DO wear warm clothing. Refreshments.
Tel: Harlech (0766) 780247. Open: Easter to October, daily. Free car park. **C.**

Jewellers are amongst the many craftsmen who demonstrate their skills at Maes Artro.

Maes Artro Tourist Village

Llanbedr

At Maes Artro there's something for all the family. The village is on a 10 acre site, set in beautiful Welsh countryside with gardens and grounds, woodland and walks, nature trail and picnic areas. The main attractions are a local sea-life aquarium, re-created old Welsh street and 1/32 scale model village. Maes Artro also has an adventure playground, 'Logopotamus' jungle and pets corner especially for the children, plus shops and restaurant.
Tel: Llanbedr (034123) 487/467. **C.**

Maesgwm Visitor Centre

Ganllwyd

Over 50 miles of paths, forest trails and tracks in the Coed y Brenin Forest have been waymarked for walkers. Pick up a guide map from the Maesgwm Visitor Centre, near Pont Dolgefeiliau on A470, n of Ganllwyd, before exploring the heart of the forest. This small but informative centre illustrates the life and work of the forest, the extraordinary rock formations and the gold mines in the area. Audio-visual programme. Picnic sites. Facilities for disabled visitors.
Open Easter to end of September. C for park park. **F.**

Cymer Abbey

A tiny, ruined abbey, on the eastern bank of the Mawddach River established by the Cistercians in the 13th century. Entrance at the old bridge over the Mawddach, at Llanelltyd, 1½m north of Dolgellau.
Open: All year, 9am to sunset. Free car park. **C.**

Cymer was the second monastery set up by the Cistercians in Gwynedd. In mediaeval times the monks wore a bleached white habit, hence they were known as the White Monks.

Porthmadog Pottery
See description on page 13.

Ffestiniog Railway
Porthmadog
See description on page 13.

Porthmadog Maritime Museum
See description on page 13.

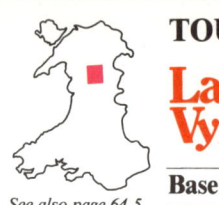

TOUR 9

Lake Vyrnwy

Base: *Welshpool*

See also page 64-5

The black and white half-timbered architecture featured here is characteristic of the Mid Wales borderlands.

Gateway to the Mid Wales Borderlands, Welshpool has long been a town of considerable importance — its Monday market received its charter in 1263. Recreational facilities in and around the town include an indoor heated swimming pool, golf course, angling on the canal and the Severn, and walking along Offa's Dyke. The Welshpool and Llanfair Railway, one of the "Great Little Trains", runs to Llanfair Caereinion. A stretch of the Montgomery Canal has been restored and re-opened near the town, and a picnic site provided on Buttington Wharf, while 1m. to the south is Powis Castle (N.T.) a mediaeval castle in formal gardens.

E.C. Thursday. M.D. Monday.
T.I.C. Vicarage Garden Car
Park. Tel. (0938) 2043 (1-12)

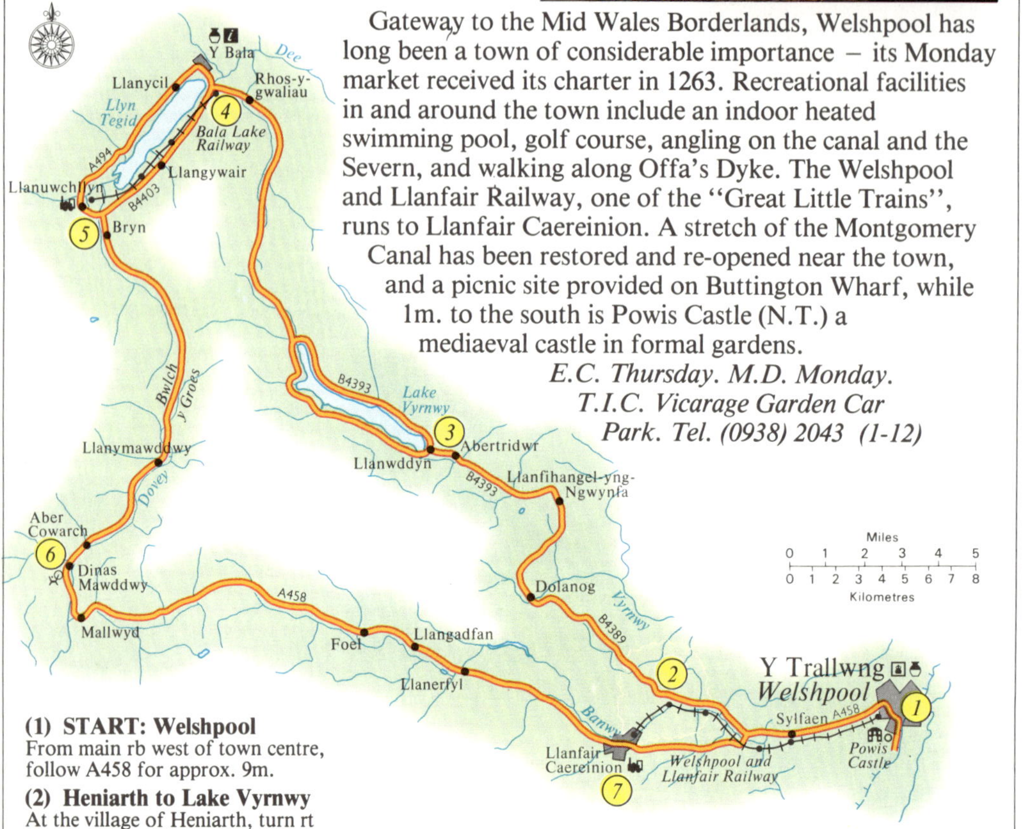

(1) START: Welshpool
From main rb west of town centre, follow A458 for approx. 9m.

(2) Heniarth to Lake Vyrnwy
At the village of Heniarth, turn rt on to B4389 for Dolanog and Llanfihangel yng Ngwynfa. ½m beyond this village a T Junction, bear l. on to B493 for Llanwddyn.

(3) Llanwddyn to Hirnant Valley
From the visitor centre, continue on B4393 on south-western side of Lake Vyrnwy or take the alternative circular route along its northern shore. From the bridge at the northern end of lake, take the unclassified road through the wooded Hirnant Valley (narrow and steep in parts). This joins the B4391, ½m west of Rhosygwaliau, to descend into Bala.

(4) Bala
From Bala take a ride on the narrow gauge railway along the lake. Alternatively drive on, along the B4403 or A494 to Llanuwchllyn.

(5) Bwlch-y-Groes
From Llanuwchllyn an unclassified road leads off the B4403 to the rt, for the very steep climb over Bwlch-y-Groes to Dinas Mawddwy on A470. This is a spectacular, mountain road, with hairpin bends. Alternative route: For those who prefer main 'A' roads to the off-the-beaten-track routes, we recommend you stay on the A494

from Llanuwchllyn to Dolgellau, then take the A470 to Dinas Mawddwy.

(6) Dinas Mawddwy to Mallwyd
From the village, take steep hill up to the A470, turning l. for a visit to Meirion Mill (½m ahead). In a further 1½m approx turn l. at the junction by Brigands Inn, on to A458, S/P Welshpool, for Llanfair Caereinion.

(7) Llanfair Caereinion
As an alternative route, from Llanfair you can return to Welshpool via Castle Caereinion on B4385.

What to see

Meirion Mill
Dinas Mawddwy

Meirion Mill, its weaving unit and extensive shop, is housed in former railway and slate quarry buildings. Welsh tapestry cloth, exclusive tweed, bedcovers, blankets and rugs, made in Pure New Wool at the mill are attractively displayed in the Mill Shop. Freshly-baked, home-made food served in the cafe. Other features of interest include a children's play garden and an excercise area for dogs.
Tel. Dinas Mawddwy (06504) 311. Open: All year. Free car park. **F.**

Vyrnwy Visitor Centre
Llanwddyn

To make the most of your tour around Lake Vyrnwy, call at the Vyrnwy Visitor Centre on your arrival in Lanwddyn. Housed in a former chapel, the centre now provides a suitable starting point for visitors exploring this area by car or on foot.

Colourful displays explain how and why the lake was created, the effect it had on the community and the natural environment, and the benefits brough by farming and forestry around the valley. The story is told with visual aids and sound effects.
Open: Easter to Spring Bank Holiday – weekends only; then daily to end of September. Free car park.

Powys Castle (N.T.)
near Welshpool

Powis is one of the most romantic castles in the Welsh Marches. Built of red sandstone, it creates an unforgettable sight, an impregnable fortress. Over the years, the castle underwent a series

of improvements, transforming it into a comfortable home. Contents include a fine collection of tapestries, furniture and paintings with works by Landscroon. The Long Gallery's almost continuous glazing gives the room a feeling of space and brightness.

The late 17th century terraced or hanging gardens are still in their original form. They are framed by the enormous clipped yews which are one of the most striking features of the magnificent grounds.
Free car park. Open: Easter to September. **C.**

Welshpool and Llanfair Railway

Unlike any of the other 'Great Little Trains of Wales', this railway runs for its duration through graceful open countryside from Welshpool to its terminus at Llanfair Caereinion, a total of 8m. Built early this century to carry country people and their produce to market, this line closed in 1956, later to be rescued by rail enthusiasts. Shop and Tea Bar at Llanfair Station. Reduced price ticket for family groups of at least two adults and two children.
Tel: Llanfair Caereinion 810441. Period of operation: Easter to mid-October (limited spring and autumn service.) **C.**

Bala Lake Railway

Bala Lake, otherwise known as Llyn Tegid, is the largest natural lake in Wales, being over 4m long and 2/3m wide. The narrow gauge Lake Railway follows a very scenic part of the old Great Western Railway line, from Bala to its terminus at Llanuwchllyn, a distance of 4½m. Light refreshments available at Llanuwchllyn Station and at the Loch Cafe, Bala.
Tel. Llanuwchllyn (067 84) 666. Period of operation: Easter to mid-October. Free car park. **C.**

Lake Vyrnwy, one of Wales's many man-made reservoirs.

TOUR 10

Cader Idris

Base: *Dolgellau*

See also page 64

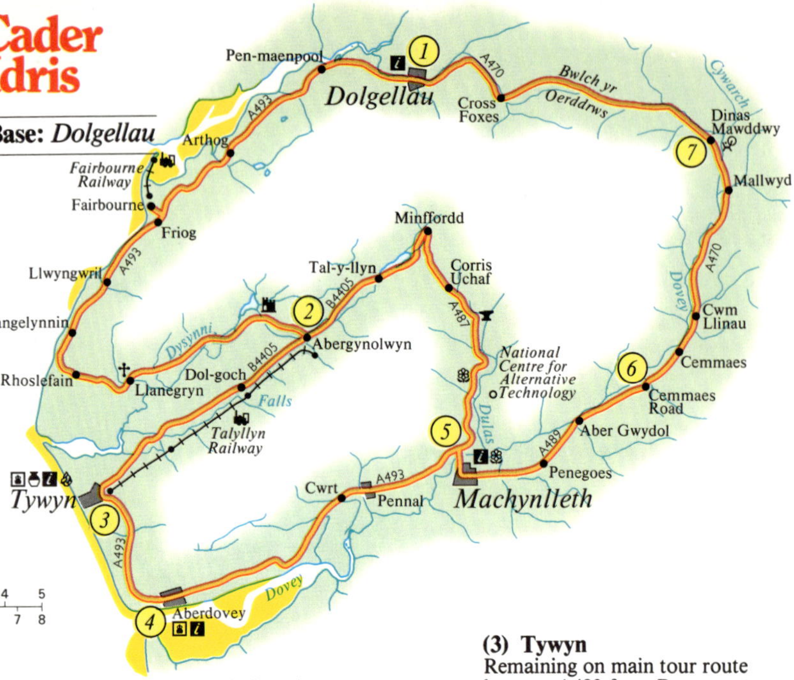

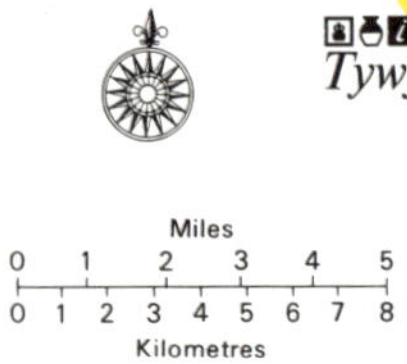

A sturdy stone-built town in the shadow of Cader Idris, yet only a short drive from the lovely Mawddach Estuary and the coast. Holiday acitivities in this area include pony trekking and riding, walking in the hills and the nearby Coed-y-Brenin forest, fishing for salmon, or just following one or two of our suggested tours to places of interest in Snowdonia. Stay on a farm, at one of the town's hotels or guest houses, or go self catering in the surrounding countryside.

T.I.C. Snowdonia National Park Visitor Centre, The Bridge. Tel. (0341) 422888(E). E.C. Wed. M.D. Fri.

(1) START: Dolgellau
From the main square follow signs for Tywyn (A493) along the south shore of the Mawddach Estuary for part of the way.

(2) Rhoslefain to Abergynolwyn
Just beyond Rhoslefain, turn l. on unclassified road to Castell-y-Bere and walk to Bird Rock.
Alternatively continue to Bryncrug and turn l. on to B4405 for drive to Dolgoch Falls, then on to Abergynolwyn, terminus of Talyllyn Railway. By keeping on this road past Talyllyn Lake you could shorten tour returning to Dolgellau via A487 (A470).

(3) Tywyn
Remaining on main tour route keep on A493 from Bryncrug to Tywyn (swimming pool, pottery) and take the Talyllyn Railway instead to the falls and Nant Gwernol. From Wharf Station continue on A493 around coast.

(4) Aberdovey
From this very attractive coastal village, follow the A493 along the Dovey Estuary to Machynlleth.

(5) Machynlleth
Beyond Pennal on A493, turn rt over arched bridge across the Dovey, into this market town. Turn l. by clock tower (car park to rt). Continue on this road (A489) S/P Newtown for approx. 7m, to the village of Cemmaes Road. Turn l. here on to A470 S/P Dolgellau.

(6) Mallwyd
In the village of Mallwyd at junction by Brigand's Inn, keep on A470 to l.

(7) Dinas Mawddwy
In approx. 2m on l. is the Meirion Woollen Mill. From here make the steady climb over the steep Bwlch yr Oerddrws Pass (A470) back into Dolgellau.
NOTE: This tour can also be shortened by returning directly to Dolgellau from Machynlleth along A487 via Corris and National Centre for Alternative Technology.

What to see

Cader Idris

For one of the best views of the Cader Idris range, a detour is necessary off the main tour route. This alternative mountain road off the A493, to the l. on leaving Dolgellau for Tywyn S/P Cader Idris, takes you to Llyn Gwernan. A well known footpath to the summit starts here. The less energetic will keep on this road, following the signs for Llynnau Cregennen – a most peaceful spot owned by the National Trust – and Arthog. Here you join the A493 for the continuation of the tour.

Ruins of Castell-y-Bere, near Tywyn.

Talyllyn Railway

From the Cambrian Coast resort of Tywyn the narrow-gauge Talyllyn Railway links up a beautiful valley to Nant Gwernol close to the foot of the Cader Idris Range. Stops at Dolgoch Falls and Abergynolwyn. Total journey time: 55 minutes each way.
Reduced price family return tickets available.
Open: Late March to early November. Limited service in early spring and autumn. Also Christmas holidays.   **C.**

Visit the railway museum at Tywyn, before taking a ride on the Talyllyn Railway.

National Centre for Alternative Technology

In these energy saving times, you may find it well worth your while to spend a little time at this most unusual attraction, the National Centre for Alternative Technology. Learn a few tips about living self-sufficiently, about solar power and wind power, about insulating your own home and growing your own produce. Exhibition room, book shop. Car park.
Off A487 at Pantperthog, north of Machynlleth.
Tel. (0654) 2400.
Open: All year.   **C.**

Learn something about more natural sources of energy at the National Centre for Alternative Technology, near Machynlleth.

Fairbourne Railway

The 'baby' of the 'Great Little Trains of Wales' family, being of only 15″ gauge. It runs for two miles alongside a sandy part of the Cambrian Coast from Fairbourne to Barmouth Ferry. Steam and diesel engines operate on this line.
Journey time: 20 minutes each way. Car park at Fairbourne. Refreshments at both stations.
Tel. Fairbourne 362.
Open: Easter week, Spring Bank Holiday to mid-October.   **C.**

Castell-y-Bere

Dramatically sited in the shadow of Cader Idris are the ruins of Castell-y-Bere. Though lacking in cunning, sophisticated devices, this native Welsh castle's remote location gave it its major defences. On minor road to Llanfihangel-y-Pennant.
Open: At any reasonable time.   **F.**

Meirion Woollen Mill

Dinas Mawddwy
See description on page 27.

TOUR 11

Wild Wales

Base: *Machynlleth*

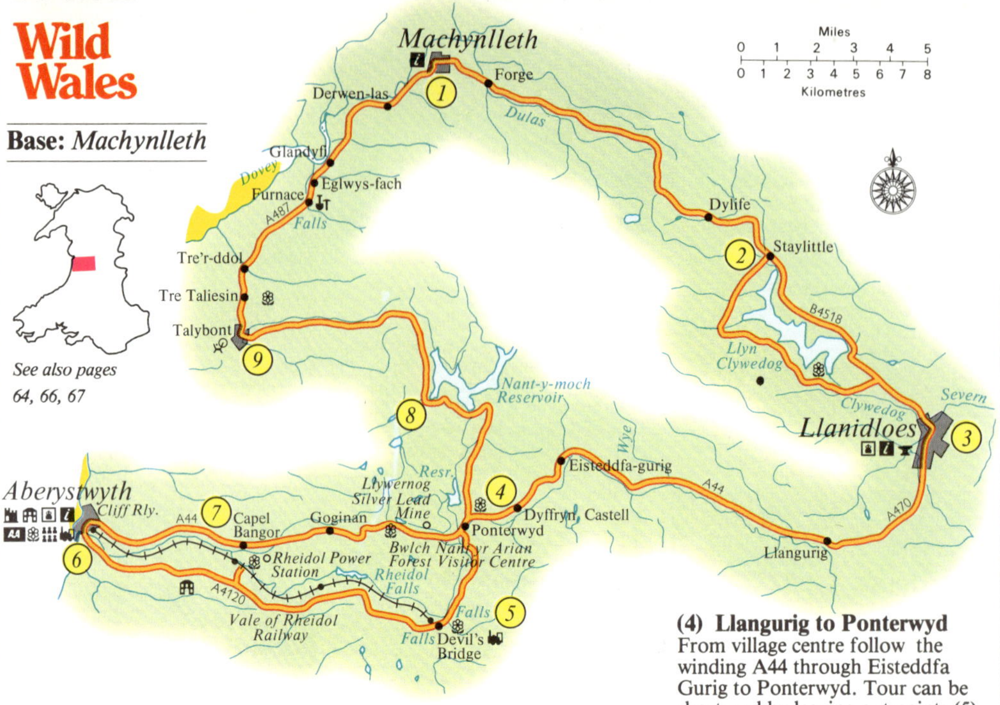

See also pages
64, 66, 67

Former coaching inns and some interesting little shops border the broad tree-lined streets of Machynlleth. Being at the junction of two major roads (A487 Dolgellau-Aberystwyth and A489), this market town for the Lower Dovey Valley also makes a perfect base for touring the Cambrian Coast, the hills of Cader

Idris and Plynlimon, and the lakelands of Mid Wales. *T.I.C. Canolfan Owain Glyndwr. Tel. (0654) 2401 (1-12). E.C. Thurs. M.D. Wed.*

(1) START: Machynlleth
Our tour, mainly on mountain roads, starts from Heol Maengwyn, Machynlleth's main street. Turn rt by Chest Hospital for steep mountain road to Dylife. 2m beyond Star Inn, at T junction with B4518, turn rt for Staylittle.

(2) Staylittle to Clywedog Reservoir
Continue on road to the east of the Clywedog reservoir, or bear rt at Staylittle on to unclassified road around lake. S/P Clywedog Reservoir. Car park by dam. Follow this road to rejoin B4518 and continue on main route to Llanidloes.

(3) Llanidloes
From town centre, head south on A470. In approx 5m at major fork in road, bear rt for Llangurig.

(4) Llangurig to Ponterwyd
From village centre follow the winding A44 through Eisteddfa Gurig to Ponterwyd. Tour can be shortened by leaving out points (5), (6), (7). Here, turn l. on to A4120. S/P Devil's Bridge.

(5) Devil's Bridge
Stay on main route to Devil's Bridge. Then continue on A4102. S/P Aberystwyth.

(6) Aberystwyth
At junction of A4120 with A487, turn rt for town centre. Car park by railway station. Leave town on A44 via Llanbadarn Fawr. S/P Llangurig.

(7) Capel Bangor to Ponterwyd
In approx 5m, beyond Capel Bangor, turn rt for visit to Rheidol Falls and Rheidol Hydro Electric Scheme Power Station. Return on to A44, for Ponterwyd, calling at Bwlch Nant yr Arian Forestry Centre or Llywernog Silver Lead Mine, en route.

(8) Nant-y-Moch
Drive on to Ponterwyd, turning l. for Nant-y-Moch Reservoirs. Follow this superb mountain road through hills and lakelands to Talybont on A487.

(9) Talybont
Turn rt here by White Lion for return to Machynlleth.

What to see

Theatr y Werin
Penglais, Aberystwyth

Evening entertainment in the form of plays, concerts, opera and ballet, is provided at Theatr y Werin, which is part of the University's Arts Centre on Penglais Hill. In the summer season the emphasis is on good family entertainment (Box Office Tel. (0970) 4218). The Arts Centre Gallery, open during evening performances (as well as daily Mon – Sat), shows regular touring exhibitions as well as a small selection of the University's ceramic collection.
Tel: (0970) 4277. Free car park.

Llywernog Silver-Lead Mine
Ponterwyd

Just off the A44, only 1m from Ponterwyd is this open-air museum, illustrating the workings of a typical lead mine in Mid Wales during the 1870s mining boom. On the 6 acre site there are water wheels, a Miners' Trail and underground tunnel, and an indoor exhibition, entitled 'The California of Wales', with imaginative re-created underground scenes.
Tel: Ponterwyd (097 085) 620. Open: Easter to end of September daily. Free car park. **C.**

Rheidol Forest Visitor Centre

At Bwlch Nant-yr-Arian, on the edge of the Cambrian Mountains, you'll find the Rheidol Forest Visitor Centre housed in an exciting new building high in the west facing hills of Plynlimon. This centre provides a fascinating introduction to the forest, and brings to life, by means of a slide show and other useful visual aids, the complete landscape of the area. Picnic site and forest trails nearby. Facilities for disabled visitors.
Open: Easter to October daily 10am-5pm (Sat. 12.30-5pm). Open until 6pm July and August. **C** *for car park.* **F.**

Rheidol Power Station
Capel Bangor

The man-made lakes at Nant-y-Moch, penned in by giant dams, are all part of the Rheidol Hydro Electric Power Scheme. Guided tours are arranged around the Power Station (daily Easter to end of October). Felin Newydd Weir, an attractively landscaped part of the complex, with viewing terrace, is quite a spectacle when floodlit in the evenings. Information Centre also on site, plus lakeside picnic site, nature trail and trout fishing in Dinas and Nant-y-Moch lakes.
Tel: Capel Bangor 667 Open: Easter to end of October. Free car park. **C.**

Vale of Rheidol Railway

British Rail's last steam operated line runs from the resort of Aberystwyth through the wooded Vale of Rheidol to its terminus at Devil's Bridge. This superb 12m long line was laid down in 1902 to carry lead ore from the Cardiganshire hill mines to waiting ships at Aberystwyth. Today the narrow-gauge railway takes visitors on the hour-long journey to scenic Devil's Bridge.
Tel: (0970) 612377. Open: Easter to early October. **C.**

At Devil's Bridge, the terminus of the Vale of Rheidol Railway, follow the nature trail down to the wooded gorge and waterfalls.

Aberystwyth Cliff Railway

The longest electric cliff railway in Great Britain carries passengers to the summit of Constitution Hill at the northern end of Aberystwyth Promenade for a 'bird's eye' view of more than 100 miles of the Cardigan Bay coastline.
Tel: Aberystwyth (0970) 617642. Open: Easter to October. **C.**

Aberystwyth's hotel lined promenade, backed by Constitution Hill.

Ceredigon Museum
Aberystwyth

This museum, of great local interest, has some outstanding exhibits, including silver coins minted in Aberystwyth Castle. One of the rooms depicts an early 19th century Cardiganshire kitchen/bedroom.
Tel: Aberystwyth (0970) 617911. Open: All year, excl. Sun., Christmas Day, Boxing Day and Good Friday, 10am – 5pm. **C.**

TOUR 12
The Marches

Base: *Newtown*

See also pages 65, 67, 68

Once a busy market town and thriving commercial centre for the woollen industry, Newtown, now being expanded, is the second new town in Wales. Reminders of its earlier industry are to be seen at the Textile Museum in Commercial Street. A good base for touring the Mid Wales borderland.

T.I.C. Town Council Buildings, The Cross. Tel. (0686) 25580 (1-12). E.C. Thurs. M.D. Tues.

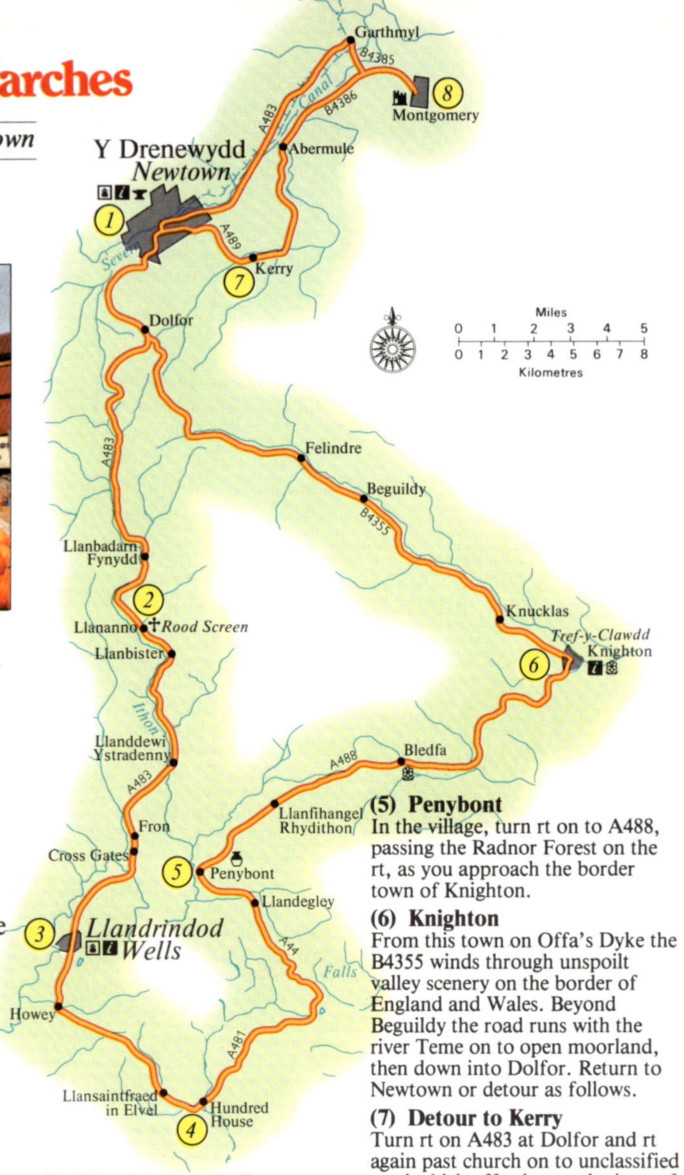

(1) START: Newtown
From Short Bridge Street, follow the road to rt S/P Llandrindod Wells (A483). Having left the town, the road follows a series of hair-pin bends and climbs to a height of 1,150ft beyond Dolfor.

(2) Llananno
Beyond Llanbadarn Fynydd the road runs parallel with the river Ithon for much of the way to Llanbister. In this pleasant valley, stop in the riverside village of Llananno, noted for its church carvings, then continue on A483. At Cross Gates rb keep forward on A483.

(3) Llandrindod Wells
Having explored this spa town, leave via Temple Street S/P A483 Builth Wells. Beyond Howey, at Crossway, turn l. on to unclassified road to Hundred House. (Alternative route via Builth A483 & A481.)

(4) Hundred House
At junction with A481, turn l. and continue through gentle hill country to junction with A44. Turn l. here for the drive into Penybont.

(5) Penybont
In the village, turn rt on to A488, passing the Radnor Forest on the rt, as you approach the border town of Knighton.

(6) Knighton
From this town on Offa's Dyke the B4355 winds through unspoilt valley scenery on the border of England and Wales. Beyond Beguildy the road runs with the river Teme on to open moorland, then down into Dolfor. Return to Newtown or detour as follows.

(7) Detour to Kerry
Turn rt on A483 at Dolfor and rt again past church on to unclassified road which affords superb views of Newtown, the Upper Severn Valley and the surrounding hills and distant mountains from its 1,196ft summit. After long descent to A489, turn rt for Kerry. Then continue on this road turning l. at junction with B4385 for Montgomery.

(8) Montgomery
At this castled town, remain on B4385 to Garthmyl turning l. on to A483 to complete the tour back to Newtown.

Map labels: Garthmyl, B4385, B4386, A483, Montgomery, Abermule, Canal, Y Drenewydd, Newtown, Kerry, Severn, A489, Dolfor, Felindre, Beguildy, B4355, A483, Llanbadarn Fynydd, Llananno, Rood Screen, Llanbister, Knucklas, Tref-y-Clawdd, Knighton, Llanddewi Ystradenny, A483, Ithon, A488, Bledfa, Fron, Llanfihangel Rhydithon, Cross Gates, Penybont, Llandegley, A44, Llandrindod Wells, Falls, Howey, A481, Llansaintfraed in Elvel, Hundred House

Miles 0 1 2 3 4 5
Kilometres 0 1 2 3 4 5 6 7 8

What to see

Newtown Textile Museum

Newtown's days as the 'Leeds of Wales' are recalled at the town's textile museum in Commercial Street. Housed in a former weaving workshop, exhibits include mill machinery, 19th century handlooms, cottage and mill shop fronts, and examples of the wool and flannel for which Newtown was once famous.

The world's first mail order business, based on Newtown's flannel industry, started at the Royal Welsh Warehouse, in the town centre (open to public).
Open: Easter to October, excl. Sun and Mon. **F.**

Tom Norton's Cycle Collection

Llandrindod Wells

The renewed interest in pedal-power brings more visitors to Tom Norton's amazing collection of old cycles and tricycles at the Automobile Palace in Temple Street. His valuable collection includes Velocipedes, Ordinaries (Penny-Farthings) and 20 other machines dating from 1867 to 1938.
Tel: Llandrindod Wells (0597) 2214. Open: Daily except Sundays and Bank Holidays. **F.**

Llandrindod Wells Museum

Originally the site museum for the excavated Castell Collen Roman fort nearby. Other exhibits, added to the collection of archaeological finds, illustrate the growth of Llandrindod Wells as a major spa town. Also on display is the Paterson collection of dolls.
Tel: (0597) 2212.
Open: All year, Mon to Sat. **F.**

Llandrindod Wells Rock Park Spa

You can 'take the waters' at this re-opened spa, set in 18 acres of wooded parkland. Llandrindod's spa waters can be sampled in authentic Edwardian surroundings in the restored Pump Room. An exhibition in the Bath House gives a fascinating insight into Llandrindod's history as a thriving spa town.
Tel: (0597) 4307. Open: Daily in summer, 10am-6pm; Weekdays in winter 10am-4pm. Free car park. **F.**

Montgomery Castle

Perched on a high rock overlooking the little border town are the scant remains of a 13th century castle built by Henry III, later occupied by the powerful Marcher family of Mortimer and the Herberts. During the Civil War it was besieged and surrendered to the Parliamentarians in 1644, who later ordered its destruction.
Open: At any reasonable time. **F.**

Around Llandrindod Wells there are still relics of the town's former days as a flourishing spa. Bottom: For a relaxing hour or two, take your rod and line to the 14 acre lake at Llandrindod.

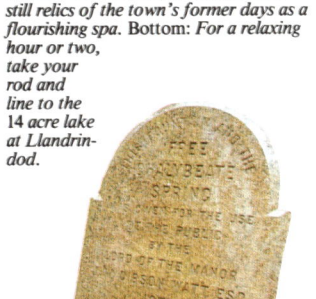

Offa's Dyke

Built by King Offa of Mercia in the 8th century to defend England from the marauding Welshmen, this dyke now forms a 167 mile long distance footpath along the borderlands from Chepstow to Prestatyn. In Mid Wales, between Knighton and Montgomery, the dyke's at its most impressive, being several feet high in parts. An information centre in the Old Primary School at Knighton will supply you with further information, including leaflets and maps.
Tel: Knighton (05472) 753.
Open: Footpath all year. Centre – seasonal opening. **F.**

Offa's Dyke Path runs the length of the Wales – England border, closely following the present day boundary.

33

TOUR 13

Elan Valley

Base: *Rhayader*

See also page 67

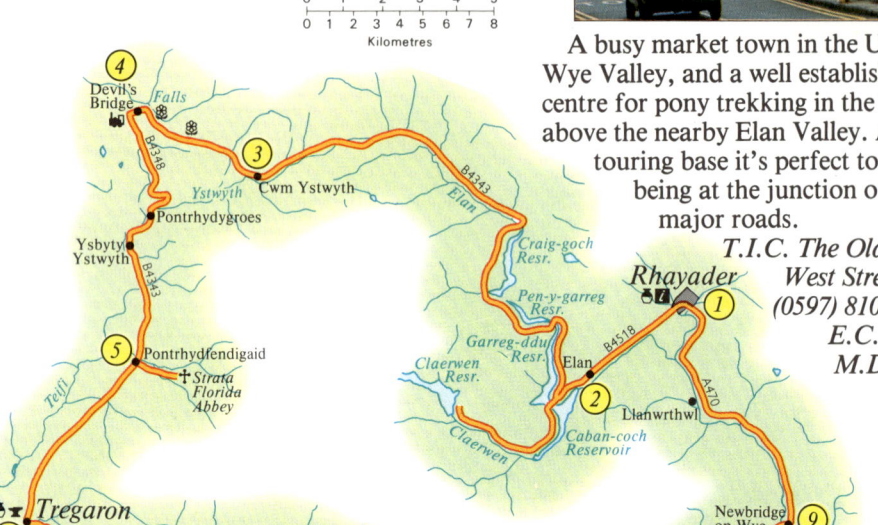

A busy market town in the Upper Wye Valley, and a well established centre for pony trekking in the hills above the nearby Elan Valley. As a touring base it's perfect too, being at the junction of two major roads.

T.I.C. The Old Swan, West Street. Tel. (0597) 810591(E). E.C. Thurs. M.D. Wed.

(1) START: Rhayader
Leave main square on B4518 S/P Elan Valley.

(2) Elan Valley
At the edge of the village, keep on unclassified road ahead to the first of the reservoirs, Caban Coch, and dam. Follow road around, crossing viaduct to l. for the drive to Claerwen Valley. Return to viaduct, and turn l. following wooded shores of Garreg-Ddu Reservoir. Continue on this unclassified road, alongside the Craig Goch Reservoirs and the Elan river, and over the remote and often bleak Ystwyth Valley.

(3) Cwmystwyth
From this almost deserted lead mining village, climb up the valley to join B4574 for Devil's Bridge.

(4) Devil's Bridge
On leaving village, where three bridges span the Mynach Gorge, turn l. on to B4343 Tregaron road, and drive through the thickly wooded Ystwyth Valley, to the lead mining village of Pontrhydygroes, then on to Pontrhydfendigaid.

(5) Detour to Strata Florida
Just beyond bridge over Teifi, at Pontrhydfendigaid, an unclassified road to l. leads to Strata Florida (see opp.). Return on same road, turning l. at bridge for pleasant drive to Tregaron. (Nature reserve on rt for much of way.)

(6) Tregaron
From square take narrow road, a former drover's route, known as the Abergwesyn Pass, over mountains to Llanwrtyd Wells.

(7) Detour to Llyn Brianne
At this point, where road crosses River Tywi, a new road to rt runs down to Llyn Brianne. Return to main route and descend into Llanwrtyd Wells.

(8) Llanwrtyd Wells
Turn l. in the town on to A483 and in approx. 4½m at Beulah, fork l. again on to B4358.

(9) Newbridge on Wye
Approaching junction with A470, turn l. for completion of tour to Rhayader.

What to see

reminders of the village's more prosperous days. During the 17th and 18th centuries it had one of the most advanced mines in Europe, producing both silver and lead. Even in Roman times lead had been mined here. From the road you can view the ruins of workshops, a dressing mill, turbine house, leats and tramways. (Do not venture on the site.)

Rheidol Valley Railway
See description on page 31.

Devil's Bridge
George Borrow, the inveterate 19th century traveller, stopped here on his journeys through 'Wild Wales'. Today's visitors will find the 300ft Mynach Falls and the three bridges spanning the wooded gorge at Devil's Bridge just as remarkable, although there may be a few more people about now, in summer in particular. Walk down the steep steps and winding paths into the gorge and the Devil's Punch Bowl or take a ride on the narrow gauge Rheidol Valley Railway into Aberystwyth.
Open: All year. Car park nearby.   **C.**

Strata Florida
Pontrhydfendigaid

The evocative ruins of the Cistercian abbey of Strata Florida stand in the most tranquil of settings in the hills of Mid Wales. Of particular interest is the splendid archway, framing the unspoilt landscape behind. Dafydd ap Gwilym, a mediaeval poet of note is reputedly buried beneath the great yew tree nearby. Budding poets often seek inspiration here!
Open: Standard Hours*
Free car park.   **C.**

This ornate archway is a noteworthy feature of the Cistercian abbey of Strata Florida, at Pontrhydfendigaid.

Abergwesyn Pass
A thrilling mountain pass over the 'Roof of Wales', through truly wild, unspoilt scenery. It was once an important road for the Welsh drovers who took their herds through often remote country to the major Smithfields of England. Narrow in parts, with passing places.

Cambrian Factory
Llanwrtyd Wells

Vistors can watch all processes from wool blending to finishing the woven cloth at this flourishing woollen mill. Welsh woolmark tweeds, travel rugs, blankets, knitting wool and garments are sold at the mill shop. ½m east of town on A483.
Tel. Llanwrtyd Wells (059 13) 211.
Open: All year. Weekdays only. Free car park.   **F.**

At many of the woollen mills of Wales visitors may watch cloths and tweeds being woven in an array of colours and designs.

Elan Valley and Claerwen Dams
Often described as the 'Lake District of Wales', the Elan Valley lakelands, built in 1904, were created by five dams forming a chain 9m long. The four main reservoirs from north to south are The Graig-goch, Pen-y-garreg, distinguished by its tiny fir-capped island, the Carreg-Ddu Reservoir, and the lowest, the Caban Coch. To the west, along a good road over the viaduct, through the Claerwen Valley is the giant 1,166ft Claerwen Dam holding back ten thousand million gallons of water. No sailing and water-sports permitted, only trout fishing (by permit) on Elan lakes.
Open: Access at any reasonable time. Free car parks.   **F.**

Cwmystwyth Lead Mine
Cwmystwyth's lunar-like landscape and the sad remains of buildings associated with the lead mining industry serve as vivid

Ceredigion

Base: *Aberaeron*

See also page 66

Aberaeron ①

Cei Newydd
New Quay ⑩

Llanarth

Synod Inn

Llangrannog ⑨

Felinfach

Mwnt ✝ ⑧

Brynhoffnant

Gwbert

Blaenannerch

Blaenporth

Llanbedr Pont Steffan
Lampeter ②

Cwm-sychpant

Llanwnnen

Poppit Sands

Aberteifi
Cardigan

Dre-fach

Pren-gwyn

Rhyd Owen

Llandudoch
St. Dogmael's

Llechryd

Cwm-cou ⑦

⑥ Cenarth

⑤ Aber-banc ③

Henllan

Cilgerran ⑦

Castell Newydd Emlyn
Newcastle Emlyn

Felindre ④

Miles
0 1 2 3 4 5
0 1 2 3 4 5 6 7 8
Kilometres

T.I.C. Harbour. Tel. (0545) 570602(E).
E.C. Thurs.

Once a busy seaport, it is now a popular sailing centre. Its colourful row of Georgian houses looks down over the boat-filled harbour, giving the harbour-side great charm and character. A well-equipped swimming-pool is open to visitors during the summer months. Although not large, Aberaeron has a good choice of guest-houses and hotel accommodation.

(1) START: Aberaeron
From town centre, take A482 S/P Lampeter.

(2) Lampeter
At T junction on main street, follow road to rt (A475) for Newcastle Emlyn. At Penrhiwllan an unclassified road to rt leads to Maesllyn Mill and Museum (see opp).

(3) Aberbanc
Continue on main route (A475) through the village of Aberbanc noted for its weaving workshop, to Newcastle Emlyn or detour as follows:

(4) Drefach Felindre
Turn l. on B4334 for Henllan, crossing A484 on to unclassified road to Museum of the Woollen Industry (see opp). Return on to main A484 for drive into Newcaslte Emlyn.

(5) Newcastle Emlyn
At bridge over Teifi, take B4333 S/P Aberporth for 1¾m to Felin Geri (on rt). Otherwise drive through town centre, following signs for Cardigan (A484) and Cenarth.

(6) Cenarth
From Cenarth Falls (see opp.) car park, continue through the Teifi Valley to riverside village of Llechryd. Turn l. here over bridge, and follow road to Cilgerran. Walk to castle. Also visit Cardigan Wildlife Park nearby, then continue on this unclassified road to junction with A478 by Penbryn Arms. Turn rt for Cardigan.

(7) Cardigan
Detour l. by bridge for St. Dogmael's and Poppit Sands. Otherwise cross bridge into town centre and follow road to l.

(8) Gwbert/Mwnt
On leaving Cardigan, turn l. on to B4548 for Gwbert. Narrow road via Verwig leads to Mwnt (not advisable in peak summer). Return to A487 via Aberporth or Blaenannerch and continue towards New Quay.

(9) Llangrannog
If time allows detour to l. for Llangrannog on B4334.

(10) New Quay
From Synod Inn drive down to New Quay, returning to A487 via B4342 and Llanarth, for journey back to base.

36

What to see

Aberaeron Sea Aquarium

Fish and other marine life found in Cardigan Bay are displayed at the Aquarium, alongside the little harbour at Aberaeron. Adjoining the centre is a cafe, honey ice cream kiosk and shop selling the locally produced Holgates honey.
Tel: (0545) 570142. Open: Easter to end of September. Car park at harbourside. **C.**

Maesllyn Mill and Museum

near Llandysul

Learn a little more about the processes of turning wool into cloth at this working mill and museum. Here too, the fascinating history of the country mill is told, aided by a very useful guide. Other features of interest at Maesllyn are the large woollen and craft shop and a nature trail. Just off tour route.
Tel: Rhydlewis (023975) 251. Open: All year. Mon − Sat 10am − 6pm. Sun 2 − 6pm. Free car park. **C.**

Felin Geri Mill

Cwm Cou

One of the last water-powered working flour mills in Wales, still using the traditional methods of grinding corn. The adjacent buildings house a small museum, a water-powered sawmill and farmyard animals. Wholemeal cookery demonstrations are given in the bakery. The cafe serves traditional farmhouse lunches and cream teas.
Tel. Newcastle Emlyn (0239) 710810. Open: Easter to September. Free car park. **C.**

Museum of the Woollen Industry

Drefach Felindre, Llandysul

A branch of the National Museum of Wales, occupying part of the Cambrian Mills, in the centre of this once important textile manufacturing region. The exhibition, with its collection of textile machinery dating back to the 18th century, traces the development of the woollen industry from the Middle Ages to the present day. 3m east of Newcastle Emlyn off the A484 (signposted).
Open: April to September, Mon − Sat. Free car park. **F.**

Cenarth Fishing Museum

Within sight and sound of the famous Cenarth Falls on the River Teifi, is Britain's first rod and line fishing museum. There are more than 300 items of fishing equipment on display − considered by fishing experts to be one of the finest collections in the world. There is also a collection of poaching tackle, as well as wildlife exhibits. Above the museum there's an art gallery exhibiting works by Welsh artists and a video showing fascinating fishing films.
Open: Easter to October, daily. Car park nearby. **C.**

Left: *Wholemeal flour produced at the Felin Geri Mill is particularly popular with visitors keen to bake their own bread.*
Below: *Maesllyn Mill and Museum, just off the main tour route.*

Cilgerran Castle

A rugged castle, built on a rocky promontory overlooking the River Teifi. This romantic setting made it the subject of a well-known painting by Richard Wilson. Cilgerran is also the setting for the annual coracle festival held each August.
Open: All year. Standard Hours. No parking.* **C.**

St. Dogmael's Abbey

near Cardigan

Monks of the French order of Tiron founded this abbey in the early 12th century. The most notable remains include the north and west walls of the nave, standing almost to their original height.
Open: At any reasonable time. Free car park. **F.**

Cardigan Wildlife Park

Cilgerran

A wildlife park showing a variety of animals, indigenous to this area in the past, including various breeds of sheep, cattle, boar, deer, horses, goats, wolves, European Bison and an aviary. The carefully planned park also provides a natural habitat for the local wildlife. A children's area has a range of smaller animals. Picnic area, adventure playground, shop and cafe.
Open: Daily. Free car park. **C.**

TOUR 15
Preseli

Base: *Fishguard*

See also page 69

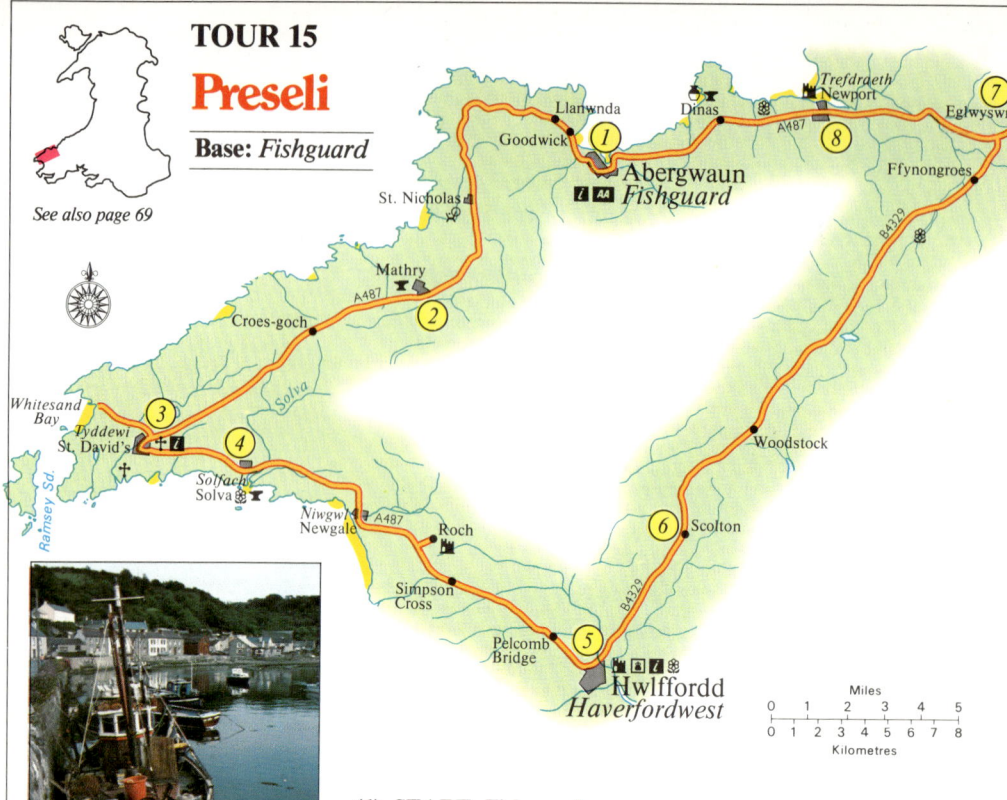

Terminal for the Irish cross-channel ferry from Rosslare and a popular centre for exploring the northern parts of the Pembrokeshire Coast National Park and the Preseli Mountains. The town of Fishguard itself stretches down to the delightful little harbour of Lower Town, used as the location for the filming of Dylan Thomas's 'Under Milk Wood'. Its attractions include a number of craft workshops.
T.I.C. Town Hall. Tel. (0348) 873484 (E). E.C. Wed. M.D. Thurs.

(1) START: Fishguard
Drive down the steep 1 in 7 hill into Lower Town, with its pretty quayside, then climb the winding road to town centre. From Main Street, follow signs for Goodwick. Detour around the Pen Caer Peninsula to St. Nicholas, rejoining A487 for rest of tour (or take direct 16m run on A487 to St. David's).

(2) Mathry
Visit the craft workshop in the village or detour down to the beach at Abercastle (1¼m). Then continue on A487.

(3) St. David's
Approaching Britain's smallest city, turn rt on to B4583 to Whitesands Bay. Return on to A487, turning rt for St. David's.

(4) Solva
3m east of St. David's still on A487 is the sheltered harbour of Solva, while a further 3m ahead on the journey to Haverfordwest, are the sandy beaches of Newgale.

(5) Haverfordwest
Leave the town on the main A40 Fishguard road, up Prendergast Hill, turning rt in ¾m to B4329.

Continue on this road for drive through rich farmland to the moorlands of Preseli.

(6) Detour to Scolton
In approx 3m detour to rt to Scolton Country Park or continue the steady climb towards the Preseli Hills. A minor road to l. leads to woollen mill at Ambleston. Further on at junction with B4313 turn rt for another short detour to Rosebush Reservoir. Return to B4329, driving over the 1,328ft summit (viewpoint) towards Eglwyswrw.

(7) Eglwyswrw
Approaching this attractive village, the B4329 joins A487. Turn l. here S/P Fishguard. In approx. 3½m turn rt for Nevern, famous for its Celtic Cross. Return to main tour route and follow A487 into Newport.

(8) Newport
Drive down to rt to Newport Sands or the sandy Parrog. Then continue along A487, with the rocky outcrops of the Preseli Hills on your l. and coast to rt.

What to see

Haverfordwest Castle and Museum

The second most important castle in the former County of Pembroke(shire), built in a strategic location 80ft above the Western Cleddau river.

The old 1820 County Gaol within the Bailey houses the Castle Museum and Art Gallery and also the Pembrokeshire Record Office. The open plan museum illustrates the history of the former Town and County of Haverfordwest, the local Military History from the Normans to the present, and also contains the regional Art Gallery. Other temporary exhibitions are a regular feature.
Tel: Haverfordwest (0437) 3708.
Open: All year, Mon to Sat except Good Friday, Christmas, Boxing and New Year's Days. Car parks nearby and at Castle. **F.**

Graham Sutherland Gallery

See description on page 41.

Preseli Crafts

All around the coast and inland in the Preseli Hills of North Pembrokeshire, there are dozens of little craft workshops (too numerous to mention individually), invariably set in beautiful surroundings. Craftsmen and women demonstrate a number of traditional skills − from pottery to candle-making, woodworking to jewellery making. Many of these are located on the map opposite. For more details get a copy of the Wales Tourist Board's guide to Crafts, available at information centres, booksellers and gift shops.

Pentre Ifan Cromlech

This fine example of a cromlech − a megalithic burial chamber − lies in the foothills of the Preseli Hills. The giant capstone 16½ft long and the three upright stones on which it is balanced are all from the hills of Preseli, which also provided the

famous 'blue stones' of Stonehenge. On minor road, off A487, at Temple Bar, 2m east of Newport.
Open: At any reasonable time. **F.**

Bishop's Palace
St. David's

Like the cathedral, the richly ornate Bishop's Palace at St. David's reflects the wealth of the church during mediaeval times. One of the most striking features of the palace, built around a central courtyard, are the arcaded parapet walls, the work of Bishop Gower.

Nearby, on the headland, are the ruins of St. Non's Chapel dedicated to St. David's mother and also St. Non's Holy Well.
Open: Bishop's Palace: Standard Hours*. Also Sun mornings. **C.**
St. Non's Chapel: at any reasonable time. **F.**

St. David's Cathedral

St. David, the patron saint of Wales, sought this quiet corner of Wales as the site of his monastery in the 6th century. It was later to become one of the greatest shrines of Christendom, with a history spanning 14 centuries. The cathedral, with its fine carving and highly ornate stonework, is a magnificent example of mediaeval architecture.
Open: All year, at reasonable times.

Tregwynt Woollen Mill
St. Nicholas

Since its early beginnings as a fulling mill in the 18th century, Tregwynt has worked continously, producing today a colourful array of tweeds, tapestries and flannels in pure new wool. 5m south-west of Fishguard. S/P off A487.
Tel: St. Nicholas (03485) 225.
Open: All year. Mon to Fri 9am-5pm Shop also open Sat and Bank Holidays 9am-5pm. Free car park. **F.**

Scolton Manor Museum
Spittal

On the B4329 Cardigan Road, 5½ m north of Haverfordwest, this new Museum of the Pembrokeshire region is situated in beautiful grounds (40 acres) which are developed as a Country Park with a Tree Trail, Nature Trail and picnic sites. Refreshments are also available. The Manor House, stables and exhibition hall contain displays of costume, photography, social and veterinary medicine, local crafts and railway history − with the 060 ST loco, 'Margaret'. An extensive archaeology gallery illustrates 'Prehistoric and Mediaeval Pembrokeshire'. There is an Audio-Visual Unit; other major displays are being developed.
Tel: Clarbeston (0437 82) 328.
Open: June to September, Tues to Sun. **F.**

Pembrokeshire Coast National Park

No tour of the Preseli coast is complete without a walk along part of the Pembrokeshire Coast Long Distance Footpath. From a point 2m north-west of St. Dogmael's, this 180m long footpath follows the coast over rocky headlands and magnificent stretches of cliffs, alternating with sandy beaches and quiet coves. Many will find the coast at its best when few people are about in spring and the headlands are ablaze with wild flowers. Leaflets and booklets about the path are available from National Park Information Centres.
Barafundle Bay on the spectacular South Pembrokeshire coast.

South Pembrokeshire

Base: *Tenby*

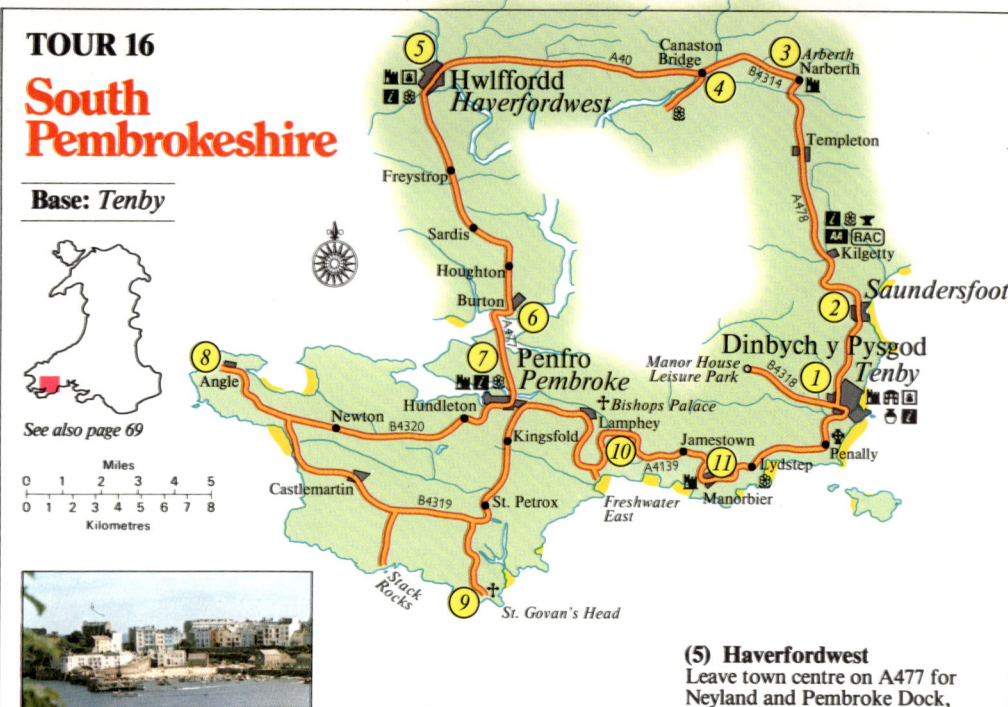

See also page 69

Miles
0 1 2 3 4 5
0 1 2 3 4 5 6 7 8
Kilometres

Tenby, undoubtedly the most impressive resort on the South Wales coast, stands on a rocky peninsula, in the Pembrokeshire Coast National Park. Its picturesque harbour, narrow mediaeval streets, its elegant rows of pastel shaded hotels and houses overlooking the sandy beaches, help preserve the distinctiveness of this ancient walled town. Tenby boasts one of the best selection of hotels and guest houses in Wales, and well-equipped holiday caravan parks, self-catering flats and chalets.

The list of attractions is just as formidable, including a Wild Life and Leisure Park, boat trips and swimming pool. *T.I.C. Guildhall, The Norton. Tel. (0834) 2402 (1-12).*

(1) START: Tenby
Head north from the centre on the A478, turning rt shortly on to B4316 for Saundersfoot.

(2) Saundersfoot
From the harbourside car park, follow the B4316 around to the A478 again, turning rt in approx. 1m at Kingsmoor Common rb. Keep straight ahead through Begelly and Templeton.

(3) Narberth
Here turn l. on to B4314 to join A40 at Robeston Wathen; then turn l. again, continuing to Canaston Bridge.

(4) Detour to Blackpool Mill
At Canaston Bridge, turn l. on to A4075, then 1st rt to Blackpool Mill. Return to A40, turning l. for Haverfordwest. In 4m detour to the l again (S/P Rhos) for the Graham Sutherland Art Gallery, then continue west on A40.

(5) Haverfordwest
Leave town centre on A477 for Neyland and Pembroke Dock, branch l. ½m beyond rb on to the recommended route through Freystrop.

(6) Burton
At this sailing centre on the Milford Haven, follow road round to the A477, turning l. over the Cleddau Bridge to Pembroke.

(7) Pembroke Dock
Continue into Pembroke town, taking the B4320 to the rt by castle.

(8) Angle
Follow the B4320 through to this western point on the South Pembrokeshire coast; then retrace your steps for 3m approx. turning l. on to B4319 through Castle Martin, back to Pembroke.

(9) Detour to St. Govan's
An unclassified road to rt leads to St. Govan's Chapel (see opp.) and the Bosherston Ponds. Return to B4319 for Pembroke or continue on unclassified road to Freshwater East, then on B4584 to Lamphey.

(10) Lamphey
Follow A4139 from Lamphey around the coast towards Tenby.

(11) Manorbier
Beyond Jameston, detour to rt to castled Manorbier, then follow B4585 around to the A4139, turning rt to complete the journey to Tenby.

What to see

Manor House Wild Life and Leisure Park
near Tenby

Spend the day in Manor House's lovely wooded grounds enjoying the wide selection of animal and bird life together with a superb collection of flowers and shrubs. For the children there's the Pet's Corner and a host of attractions in the Adventure Playground including radio-controlled tanks and boats, roundabouts, the giant 'Astraglide' slide and go-kart track. Other attractions on site include a huge model railway exhibition, picnic areas, aquarium, tropical plant house, gift shop, refreshments and a daily falconry display (except Saturdays).
Tel: Carew 201. Open: Easter to October daily. Free car park. **C.**

Tenby Museum

A museum of local history showing the archaeological and historical remains of former Pembrokeshire and Tenby, in particular. The Zoological Department has a collection of birds, mammals and sea shells. Two new galleries house special exhibitions.
Tel: (0834) 2809. Open: All year. **C.**

Tudor Merchant's House
Tenby

This exceptional mediaeval town house, near the harbour of Tenby is a reminder of the town's seafaring days in the Tudor period. Flemish influences can be seen in the early wall paintings in fresco on the interior. Owned by the National Trust.
Tel: Tenby (0834) 2279. Open: Easter to end of September. **C.**

Blackpool Mill and Caves
near Narberth

Blackpool Mill, on the south bank of the Eastern Cleddau, is one of the finest examples in Britain of a corn grinding mill. Within the attractive mill building there's an interesting display of old accounts, bills and wages. The artificial caves contain prehistoric animals and a legendary Welsh dragon.
Open: Easter to September, daily. **C.**

Graham Sutherland Gallery

Graham Sutherland, one of Britain's most distinguished artists, found inspiration for many of his paintings in the Pembrokeshire countryside which he first visited in 1934. As a token of his appreciation he and his wife established a Foundation and gallery, in 1976, with the largest collection of Sutherland works available to the public – works in mixed media, sketches, watercolours, oils, lithographs, aquatints and etchings. The Foundation is a charity. The grounds of Picton Castle are also open to visitors (charge).
Tel: Rhos (043786) 296. Open: 1 April to 30 September except Mon. Special arrangements for parties. Car park free. **C.**

Haverfordwest Castle and Museum

See description on page 39.

Pembroke Castle

Towering above the narrow streets of Pembroke, and overlooking the Milford Haven are the robust battlements of the 11th century castle. The mighty gatehouse, a fine example of the mediaeval architect's skill and cunning, withstood a number of sieges during the castle's turbulent history.
Open: All year. Daily Easter to September. Mon – Sat, October 1 to Easter. **C.**

St. Govan's Chapel

52 steps down a rugged cliff on the Pembrokeshire coast lead to the tiny 13th century church of St. Govan's. A doorway in the south-west corner leads to a holy well.
Access when firing range is open. Times at Bosherston P.O. **F.**

Lamphey Bishop's Palace

Lamphey, with its ornate parapets, orchards and once luscious gardens, gives us a hint of the wordly lives of the church prelates in mediaeval times. It was built as a country seat for the Bishops of St. David's.
Car park. Open: Standard Hours* **C.**

Manorbier Castle

Manorbier was described as the 'most delightful part of Pembroke' and the 'pleasantest spot in Wales' 800 years ago. Today it is still just as delightful, in an unspoilt part of the Pembrokeshire coast. The baronial hall and state apartments testify to its former grandeur as a nobleman's seat as well as a sturdy Norman stronghold.
Open: Easter; then Spring Bank Holiday to end of September. **C.**

Pembroke's defensive site, protected by water and stone.

TOUR 17

Hills & Forests

Base: *Llandovery*

See also pages
67, 70-1

Miles
0 1 2 3 4 5
0 1 2 3 4 5 6 7 8
Kilometres

An important market town on the A40, a former coaching route into West Wales. The town comes alive on Fridays for the weekly livestock market, when farmers and dealers throng the narrow streets and square, just as the drovers did before them in the last century. Llandovery's hotels, many of them old coaching inns of character, are of a good standard. One of them even has a four-poster bed where Lord Nelson reputedly slept.

T.I.C. Brecon Beacons National Park Centre, Central Car Park, Broad Street. Tel. (0550) 20693 (E). E.C. Thurs. M.D. Fri.

(1) START: Llandovery
At western end of the main street, turn l. on to A4069, through rich farming country on south side of the Tywi Valley.

(2) Llangadog
In centre of village by Castle Hotel, follow road to l. S/P Gwynfe, Llanddeusant. At cross-roads by Three Horse Shoes, keep straight ahead (S/P Brynaman) still following the A4069 through a wooded gorge, making the steep, winding ascent on to the open moorland of the Black Mountain.

(3) Black Mountain Viewpoint
At this point, over 1,600ft high, pull into the car park for spectacular views of the Brecon Beacons, then drop into Brynaman turning rt at rb.

(4) Brynaman to Trapp
Take the narrow road (rough in parts) to rt by Post Office (S/P Llandeilo) to Trapp. From bridge detour to rt to Castell Carreg Cennen, then follow unclassified road to Ffairfach. At crossroads on A40 turn rt to Llandeilo.

(5) Llandeilo
From town centre, return to Ffairfach; turn rt on to A476 S/P Llanelli, and in ¾m turn rt again on to B4300 for a relaxing drive through the green lush Tywi Valley.

(6) Dryslwyn Castle
In 4m turn rt for Dryslwyn Castle, dramatically sighted above the river. Return on to the B4300, with Paxton's Tower on the hill above and turn rt.

(7) Nantgaredig
In approx. 4m turn rt for Nantgaredig, crossing the A40 on to the B4310. This road runs through the Cothi Valley up into the forested slopes of Brechfa and Abergorlech (**Alternative:** *detour into Carmarthen via Abergwili.*)

(8) Llansawel
Here, at junction of B4310 and B4337 turn rt for visit to Talley Abbey, or drive straight across to join B4302, near Crugybar, (2½m). This road meets the A482. Turn rt for Llanwrda, then back to Llandovery along A40.

(9) Pumsaint
But if time allows detour 1½m to l. for visit to Roman Gold Mines at Dolau Cothi, then return to Llandovery as suggested.

What to see

Though so much of Talley Abbey's remains have been swept away, the central tower of the church stands almost to its original height.

Castell Carreg Cennen, near Llandeilo, dramatically sited overlooking the lush Tywi Valley

Castell Carreg Cennen
near Llandeilo

Dramatically sited on a rocky outcrop 300ft above the scenic Tywi Valley and overlooking the Black Mountain, the present castle dates from the 13th and 14th century. A vaulted passage leads to a fascinating cave beneath the castle, which provides an air of excitement for children.
Access down footpath from car park.
Open: All year. Any reasonable time.
Free car park.   **C.**

Dryslwyn Castle

Like Castle Carreg Cennen, Dryslwyn Castle stands in a commanding position on a hill overlooking the Tywi Valley. In the 13th century it was held by the Lord Rhys, one of the most powerful Welsh rulers during the reign of Henry II. Beneath the towering remains is a pleasant picnic site on the bank of the Tywi river.
Limited parking.

Carmarthen Museum
Abergwili

Set in 2 acres of parkland, in the former Bishop's Palace at Abergwili is this informative and well laid out museum, illustrating the cultural life and history of the Carmarthen region. Displays relate to the rural industries of the area, including dairy farming and coracle making, geology and archaeology, Welsh culture, folk life and local military history. The original chapel of the Bishop's Palace has also been retained here, intact. Within the grounds there's a lovely walk, with picnic areas provided. Information Centre.
Tel: Carmarthen (0267) 31691.
Open: All year. Mon – Sat, excl. Good Friday, Christmas and New Year. Free car park.   **F.**

Gwili Railway

Wales's first standard gauge steam railway runs from Bronwydd Arms, on A484, just north of Abergwili, following part of the old Carmarthen-Aberystwyth line, through the Gwili Valley. Off the main tour route. Picnic area. Refreshments. Souvenir Shop.
Tel: Maesteg (0656) 732176
*Free car park. Limited Service.***C.**

Talley Abbey

Detour off the main route down the B4302 to the remains of 12th century Talley Abbey, in a beautiful setting at the head of the Talley Lakes. Though the remains are scanty, the beauty and the peaceful atmosphere of their location make the visit worthwhile.
Open: All year. Standard hours*
Free car park.   **C.**

Roman Gold Mines
Dolau Cothi

Gold was mined by the Romans here in Pumsaint, most probably to provide gold bullion for the Imperial Mints in France and Rome. Two short waymarked trails of 1m and ½m each, explore this fascinating site on National Trust land, showing aqueduct systems, opencast workings and Roman adits. Start at Ogofau Lodge, on Cwrt y Cadno road.
Tel: Pumsaint 556. Open: All year. Special mine tours daily, 11am – 5.30pm, July to September. Free car park.

Abergorlech Forest Walk

From the car park in the village of Abergorlech, on B4310, a 1½ – 2m walk takes you into the Brechfa Forest, which clothes the northern slopes of the lovely Vale of Cothi.
Open: All year. Free car park. **F.**

TOUR 18
Brecon Beacons

Base: *Brecon*

*See also pages
67-8, 71-2*

Market town and main touring centre for the 519 square miles of the Brecon Beacons National Park. Of interest in the town is the Brecknock Museum, Regimental Museum, and 14th century cathedral dominating the narrow streets. For the energetic there's a swimming pool, golf, tennis, bowls, boating and a number of pony trekking centres in the locality.

T.I.C. Market Car Park. Tel. (0874) 2485 (E). Also Brecon Beacons National Park Office, Glamorgan Street. Tel. (0874) 4437 (1-12). E.C. Wed. M.D. Fri.

(1) START: Brecon
Leave the town on the west bound A40 S/P Llandovery.

(2) Sennybridge
In 8½m turn l. on to A4067 S/P Swansea, Ystradgynlais.

(3) Defynnog to Heol Senni
At Defynnog, 1½m ahead, bear l. on to A4215. S/P Merthyr Tydfil and Libanus, and in approx. 1m bear rt for Heol Senni. Here turn rt for mountain road to Ystradfellte (a narrow road with passing places, providing marvellous views of Beacons and Forest Fawr). Picnic site on l. at Blaen Llia.

(4) Ystradfellte
Turn l. on village square opposite Post Office for Penderyn.

(5) Penderyn
A l in 7 hill joins A4059, 1½m north of Penderyn. Turn rt here, and in the village, by Lamb Hotel, turn l. S/P Cwm Cadlan – a superb unfenced mountain road which runs down into Coed Taf Fawr Forest by the Llwyn-Onn Reservoir. (Picnic sites and forest walks on rt.)

(6) Llwyn-Onn Reservoir
At T. Junction, by lake, turn rt and follow road around reservoir, turning rt on to A470.

(7) Cefn Coed y Cymmer
Here in 2¼m, turn l. for Pontsticill, following shores of Taf Fechan

Reservoir. A new narrow gauge railway runs to the former B.R. station at Pontsticill which overlooks the reservoir dam. Continue on this unclassified road through the Taf Fechan Forest, where there are car parks, picnic sites and forest walks, steadily climbing to the 1,400ft summit for wide views of the Beacons. The tour now descends past the Talybont Reservoir, into the canal-side village of the same name.

(8) Talybont
Cross over the canal and turn rt on B4558.

(9) Llangynidr
Turn rt by Coach and Horses Inn, and continue for 1m, through the village, turning rt onto B4560 (S/P Beaufort) for 2m for outstanding views of the Beacons. Return on same route to Llangynidr and turn rt on to B4560 which joins A40 at Bwlch. Turn l. then rt in ½m on to B4560 (S/P Talgarth).

(10) Llangorse Lake
In village of Llangorse, turn l. by Ellesmere Trekking Centre for lakeside. Return along this lane, turning l. along unclassified road through Llanfihangel Talyllyn, which joins A40 for the drive back to Brecon.

What to see

Wales's newest narrow-gauge line, the Brecon Mountain Railway.

As there's so much to see and do in the Brecon Beacons we have included two tours here. This second tour, which keeps mostly to the easy-to-follow main roads takes you across fabulous motoring country, with panoramic views of the mountains almost round every corner. It also takes you to some of the National Park's well-known attractions, including the Dan-yr-Ogof Caves at Abercraf, featured below, and the nearby Craig-y-Nos Country Park, not forgetting the Mountain Centre at Libanus.

Dan-yr-Ogof Showcaves
near Abercraf (Abercrave)
The Dan-yr-Ogof Caves are on the A4067 near Abercraf. Guided tours take visitors into the largest showcave complex in Western Europe, with breathtaking formations built up over thousands of years. More recent additions include an amazing Dinosaur Park, the Bone Cave illustrating cave occupation through the ages to Roman times, presented by means of effective re-created scenes, and the Geological Trail. Small museum, restaurant, shop, information centre, motel, award-winning self-catering apartments, caravan park, camping all part of complex. Ample parking.
Tel: Abercraf (0639) 730284/730693. Open: Easter to October, daily. **C.**

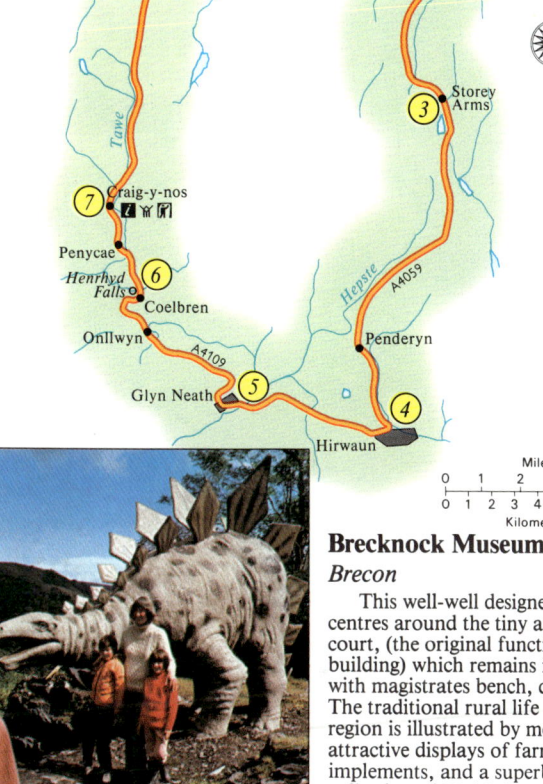

One of the dinosaurs at the Dan-yr-Ogof Caves.

Brecon Mountain Railway
Pant, near Merthyr Tydfil
This, the newest narrow-gauge 'Great Little Train' follows a 2 mile route from its Pant terminus into the foothills of the Brecon Beacons. From its beautiful lakeside halt at Pontsticill, many attractive walks can be taken.
Tel: Merthyr Tydfil (0685) 4854. Open: Daily, Spring Bank Holiday to mid-September. Weekends Easter, then May Day to Spring Bank Holiday and mid-September to New Year. **C.**

Brecknock Museum
Brecon
This well-well designed museum centres around the tiny assize court, (the original function of the building) which remains intact, with magistrates bench, dock etc. The traditional rural life of the region is illustrated by means of attractive displays of farm implements, and a superb collection of Welsh love spoons.
Tel: Brecon (0874) 4121
Car park off main street.
Open: All year. **F.**

South Wales Borderers Regimental Museum
Brecon
Visitors who saw the film 'Zulu' will be fascinated by the display relating to the famous Battle of Isandhlwana and Defence of Rorke's Drift at this museum. As well as the Victoria Crosses awarded to men of the South Wales Borderers who fought in these bloody battles, there are over 1,000 other medals and militaria on display.
Tel: Brecon (0874) 3111 Ext 310. Free car park at the Watton, on entering town from south. Open: All year.

TOUR 19

Black Mountains

Base: *Abergavenny*

See also pages 68, 72

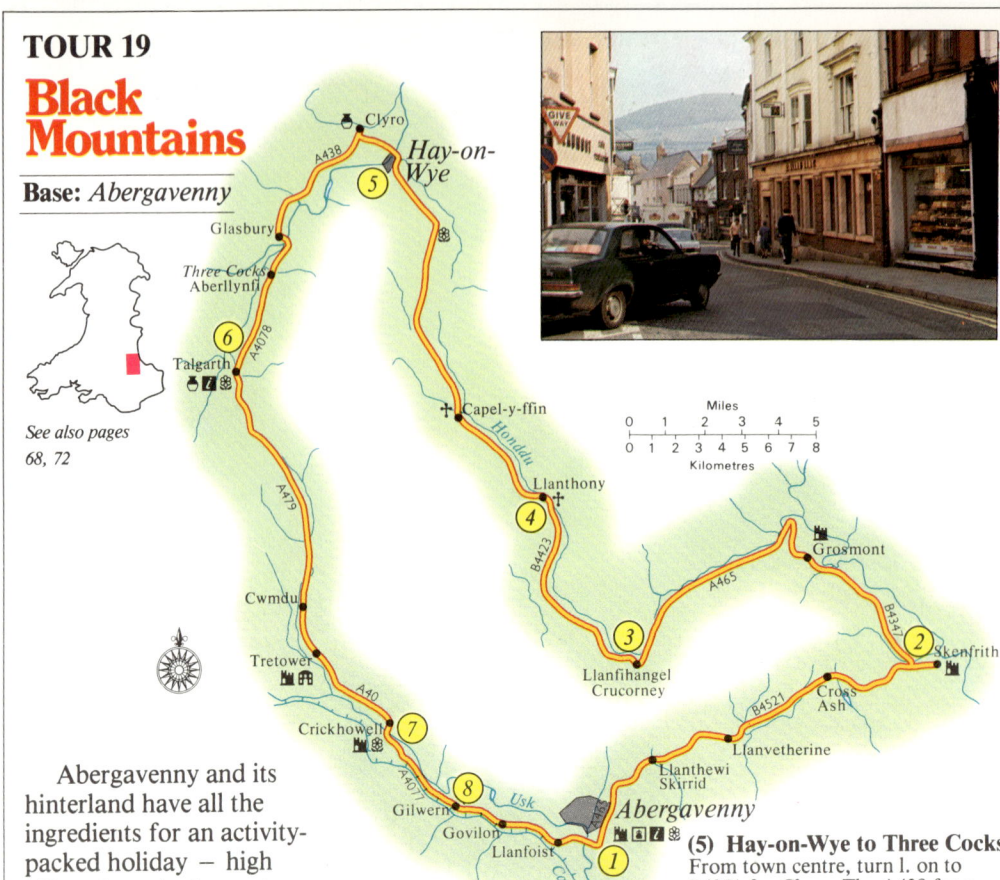

Abergavenny and its hinterland have all the ingredients for an activity-packed holiday – high hills, a broad salmon river, canal cruising, pony trekking, craft shops and workshops, historic houses and castles. Other attractions within the town include a Leisure Centre, swimming pools and bowling greens in Bailey Park, museum and a Town Trail.

T.I.C. Lower Monk Street. Tel. (0873) 3254 (E). E.C. Thurs. M.D. Tues., Fri.

(1) START: Abergavenny
From Monk St junction, opp. T.I.C. turn l. In approx. ½m turn rt on to B4521 S/P Skenfrith. This is a good B road, running through gentle countryside, to the picturesque village of Skenfrith.

(2) Skenfrith
From the village return on same route, B4521, for 1m, turning rt for Grosmont on B4347. A few hundred yds from the pretty village square, turn l. down unclassified road to Llangua (1½m) and hence to junction with A465. Here, take l. turn S/P Abergavenny. Follow this main road for 8 miles approx.

(3) Llanfihangel Crucorney
Beyond the Skirrid Inn, take road to rt (B4423) S/P Cwmyoy/ Llanthony. This is a *narrow* road with passing places, to the serene Llanthony Abbey (see opp).

(4) Llanthony to Hay-on-Wye
From Llanthony, the road narrows further, becoming steeper, beyond Capel-y-ffin, as you climb the Gospel Pass. Park at the top, by Hay Bluff, for panoramic views. As you descent from mountain-road, turn rt onto B4350 for Hay town centre.

(5) Hay-on-Wye to Three Cocks
From town centre, turn l. on to B4351 for Clyro. The A438 from here, runs down into Glasbury and Three Cocks. ½m beyond village take the A4078 to the l. S/P Talgarth 2m.

(6) Talgarth to Tretower
In Talgarth follow A479. S/P Abergavenny/Crickhowell.

(7) Tretower to Crickhowell
On route, visit Tretower Court and Castle, on r.h.s., then proceed on A479 to junction with A40 at Nantyffin Cider Mill. Turn left here and follow A40 to Crick-howell. Bear rt on to A4077 S/P Gilwern.

(8) Gilwern to Abergavenny
Follow A4077, which runs parallel with the Monmouthshire and Brecon Canal for much of the way, to Gilwern. From major rb 1m east of Gilwern, follow the A465 Heads of the Valleys road back into Abergavenny.
For a quieter alternative route, from the rb take B4246 through Govilon, Llanfoist and Llanellen, returning via A4042.

What to see

Llanthony Abbey

Few people drive through the remote Vale of Ewyas, in the Black Mountains from Abergavenny to Hay-on-Wye, without stopping to wonder at the majestic ruins of Llanthony Abbey. Graceful arches and the ruined nave give a hint of its original splendour. The former Priest's House is now a hotel. Useful leaflet available from National Park Information Centres.
Open: At any reasonable time. Free car park. **F.**

The majestic remains of Llanthony Abbey.

Capel-y-ffin Monastery

Four miles further up the Gospel Pass from Llanthony, is another monastery, dating from the last century. Father Ignatius, who came to Capel-y-ffin to 'serve the Lord in solitude', laid the foundation stone in 1870 and monastic life continued there until 1908. Picnic tables provided nearby.
Open: Any reasonable time. Limited parking.

Hay-on-Wye Bookshop

Richard Booth's empire of secondhand bookshops in the border town of Hay-on-Wye, is the largest in the world. Thousands of books fill many of the town's buildings, the main shop being The Limited, Lion Street.
Tel: Hay-on-Wye (0497) 820322. Open: All year. **F.**

Abergavenny Castle and Museum

A small museum full of interest housed in an extension to a 19th century hunting lodge built on the ruins of the town's 12-13th century castle. Local history is the main theme of the museum. Of special note is the re-created Welsh kitchen and display of coachbuilding in Abergavenny.
Tel: Abergavenny (0873) 4282. Open: All year. Closed Sundays — November to March. **C.**

Most of the exhibits at Abergavenny's museum relate to the local history of the area.

Grosmont Castle

Built in 1201 as part of a defensive triangle of castles on the border between England and Wales.
Open: At any reasonable time. **F.**

Tretower Court and Castle

Tretower Court is a perfect example of a stately home of the late mediaeval period, with a first floor gallery of particular note. Two ranges of rooms are built around a central courtyard with a curtain wall and gatehouse serving as a defence against marauders. 200 yards, north-west are the remains of an earlier motte and bailey.
Tel: Bwlch (0874) 279. Open: All year. Standard Hours. * *Limited parking.* **C.**

Wye Pottery
Clyro

Visit the Wye Pottery in the centre of Clyro and watch Adam Dworski at work. Here he produces a distinctive type of earthenware

pottery, using majolica and brushwork decoration, as well as unusual figures, plaques and pots in oxidised stoneware.
Tel: Hay-on-Wye (0497) 820510. Open: All year. Free car park. **F.**

Skenfrith was once an important strategic site.

Skenfrith Castle

13th century Skenfrith was linked with nearby Grosmont and White Castle, which together controlled the area between the Black Mountains and the Wye. The castle remains are in a really peaceful setting on the west bank of the River Monnow, almost to their original height. Guidebooks available at the local post office. A few yards away is an old Flour Mill, still using water power.
Open: At any reasonable time. **F.**

Llanfihangel Court
near Abergavenny

One of the most outstanding country houses in Gwent, of Tudor origin with a beautifully furnished interior, remodelled during the 16th and 17th centuries. Accessible off A465, at Llanfihangel Crucorney.
Tel: Crucorney (087 382) 217. **C.**

TOUR 20
Valleys of the Usk and Wye

Base: *Chepstow*

See also page 72

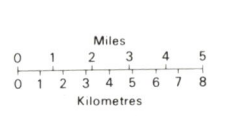

Miles
0 1 2 3 4 5
0 1 2 3 4 5 6 7 8
Kilometres

Only 1½ miles from the Severn Bridge, and just off the M4 motorway is this historic town of Chepstow. Dominating the cliffs above the River Wye is its great Norman Castle, which was a major centre of military and administrative power during the reign of the marcher lords. Other attractions within the town include a museum of local history, an impressive cast iron bridge over the Wye, the famous Chepstow Racecourse and St. Pierre's Golf Club.
T.I.C. The Gatehouse, High Street. Tel. (02912) 3772 (E). E.C. Wed.

(1) START: Chepstow
Leave town centre on A466, following signs for Monmouth. 1m beyond St. Arvan's, note car park on l. to Wyndcliff Walk for views of Tintern Forest and the Wye. Continue on the winding A466 to Tintern.

(2) Tintern
Arriving in village centre, turn rt. into the Abbey car park. Picnic areas provided nearby. Beyond Tintern the forest thins out a little to reveal views of the meandering Wye on your left. Follow the A466 through the Wye Valley to Monmouth.

(3) Monmouth
Cross the main road bridge into Monmouth town centre. Leave Monmouth on A40. S/P Abergavenny/Raglan.

(4) Raglan
At Raglan detour off A40 (dual carriageway) for visit to castle. Return on to A40, in direction of Abergavenny. Take the "old" main road west (*not* the new dual carriageway), turning l. on to unclassified road, just beyond Clytha Arms. Continue on this road, to join A471 at Llancayo. Turn l. here for Usk.

(5) Usk and Wolvesnewton
For detour to Wolvesnewton Folk Museum and Craft Centre, follow road to rt. from Priory Church, driving under flyover, bearing l. for Llangwm on to narrow road. At Llangwm, bear rt. at T junction, and first l. for Wolvesnewton. Alt. route: Take B4235 S/P Gwernesney from A472 near major rb. 1½m east of town centre. Staying on main tour, cross the bridge over the Usk, turning l. for Caerleon, via Llanbadoc and Llangybi.

(6) Caerleon
Follow the one-way system around, turning l. for Roman Amphitheatre. Free car park nearby. Roman Legionary Museum is on main road. Continue main tour, turning l. for Christchurch at bridge over the Usk (by pub). At main road junction turn l. and continue to large rb., taking Langstone turn-off here on to A48.

(7) Penhow
Follow A48 towards Chepstow. Along this road at Penhow a turning to the rt. takes you to Penhow Castle (see opp.). For a picnic detour off this road via Llanfair Discoed to the Wentwood Reservoir and Forest. Otherwise continue on A48 to Chepstow.

(8) Caerwent
At Caerwent turn rt. for visit to Roman Remains.

What to see

Chepstow Castle

Norman Lord William Fitz-Osborn built this massive stronghold, with its Great Tower, as a base for his advances into the Welsh kingdom of Gwent in the 11th century.
Open: All year. Standard Hours.* Also S.M.
Free car park overlooks the castle. **C.**

Chepstow Museum

Gwy House, Bridge Street

A museum illustrating the history of Chepstow and the surrounding area. Exhibits illustrate the town's past importance as a port, with wine trade, shipbuilding and salmon fishing, plus local crafts and industries.
Open: March to October. Mon. – Sat., 11am-5pm (closed lunchtime). Sun. 2-5pm. **C.**

Tintern Abbey

Set amidst some of the most splendid scenery to be found anywhere in Britain are the majestic remains of the Cistercian abbey at Tintern. A small exhibition tracing the history of the Abbey and its restoration is housed in a purpose-built visitor centre to the rear of the Abbey Car Park. Also housed here is a Tourist Information Centre.
Open: Standard Hours.* Also S.M. **C.**

Monmouth Museum

Market Hall, Priory Street

Admiral Lord Nelson briefly visited Monmouth in 1802, on his way to Pembrokeshire. As a permanent reminder of his visit Lady Llangattock (Charles Rolls' mother) made a collection of articles connected with the Admiral, now on display in the Nelson Museum. The small but

lively Local History Centre opposite is also well worth a visit.
Open: All year. **C.**

The Monnow Bridge

Monmouth

Monmouth's fortified gateway spanning the river Monnow — the only surviving example of its kind in Britain — provided added protection for the castle in mediaeval times.

The Monnow Bridge is still in use today as an entry point into the town's main thoroughfare.

Monmouth Castle

Monmouth Castle was one of the chain of castles built by William FitzOsborn in the 12th century. Harry of Monmouth, who later became Henry V, was born here.
Open: Exterior only, at any reasonable time. **F.**

Raglan Castle

Dating mainly from the mid 15th century, the sturdy Raglan Castle is noted for its impressive Great Tower of Gwent, built to a hexagonal plan, and surrounded by a moat. Spacious halls and state apartments, a buttery, pantry and kitchen tower help the visitor conjure up a complete picture of Raglan as an occupied castle of splendour.
Open: All year. Standard Hours.* Also S.M. **C.**

Caerleon Roman Amphitheatre and Museum

Caerleon, the Roman Legionary fortress of Isca and one of the three principal military bases in Britain, is one of our great Roman sites. The most memorable of all the ruins is the mangificent amphitheatre, used 2,000 years ago to accommodate crowds of up to 6,000 people. On the main road is the Legionary Museum, a branch archaeological gallery of the National Museum of Wales.
Open: All year. Standard Hours.* Also S.M. **C.**

Penhow Castle

Wales's oldest lived in castle, Penhow lay neglected for several centuries, until recent restoration by the present owner. Today's visitors are taken on a journey through history from the 17th century kitchen to the 12th century ramparts (with views of three counties), from the Great Hall of the 15th century with its newly-constructed minstrel gallery to the homely Victorian house-keeper's room.
Tel: Penhow (0633) 400800.
Open: Easter to September.
Limited free parking. **C.**

Caerwent Roman Site and Walls

Remains of a Roman city founded about AD75 as the self-governing capital of the Silures, including the substantial city walls which rise to a maximum height of 17ft.
Open: At any reasonable time. **F.**

Wentwood Forest

Reached by a minor road off the A48, near Penhow, is the 3,000 acre Wentwood Forest. Within the forest there are 5 waymarked walks and picnic sites provided, as well as a wayfaring course.
Open: All year. Free car park.

The Model Farm Folk Collection and Craft Centre

Wolvesnewton, near Usk

As well as an extensive folk collection, including items used in every-day and agricultural life since the days of Queen Victoria, there are also thriving craft workshops here. The mill houses changing exhibitions.
Tel: Wolvesnewton (029 15) 231.
Open: Easter week then Sat., Sun. and Mon. to end of June, 11am-6pm. July to September daily, 11am-6pm. October and November, Sun. only, 2-5.30pm. Free car park. **C.**

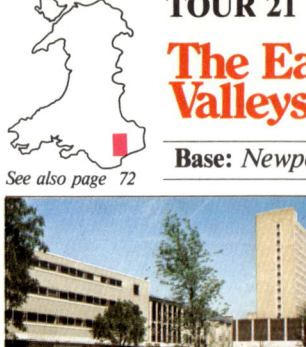

TOUR 21

The Eastern Valleys

Base: *Newport*

See also page 72

From the town of Newport, or even from nearby Cardiff, discover the industrial heritage of Gwent's Eastern Valley and the Rhymney Valley. Newport, which developed with the growth of industry, is just off the M4 motorway. Two town walks will take you to most of the sites of interest, including the remains of Newport Castle and St. Woolos Cathedral. Leaflets are available from the T.I.C. South-west of the town is Tredegar House Country Park, where children are particularly well catered for.

T.I.C. Newport Museum and Art Gallery, John Frost Square. Tel. (0633) 842962 (1-12).
E.C. Thurs. M.D. Wed., Fri., Sat.

(1) START: Newport
From town centre, head west for M4 junction with A467. Continue on A467 S/P Risca, turning rt. in approx. ½m at Henllys S/P, for Fourteen Locks Interpretive Centre and Picnic Site.

(2) High Cross to Cwmcarn
From the Centre, return to A467, turning rt. for Risca and Crosskeys. 1m further up valley, bear l. on to B4591, for Cwmcarn Scenic Forest Drive.

(3) Cwmcarn via Crumlin
Following Scenic Drive, return to A467, continue northwards through Newbridge to Crumlin. Here turn rt. by Navigation Hotel on to A472 S/P Pontypool/Blaenavon.

(4) Pontypool to Blaenavon
In approx. 6m arrive in Pontypool town centre. In the main street fork to the rt. on A4043 for Cwmavon and Blaenavon.

(5) Blaenavon
See the Blaenavon Ironworks in North Street, then follow B4246 — an open mountain road over the Blorenge (detour for Big Pit). On a clear day you'll get extensive views of the Brecon Beacons from this road. Drive down into the canal-side village of Govilon. West of village at major rb., take road to rt. for Gilwern.

(6) Gilwern
From this village on the Monmouthshire and Brecon Canal return on to the fast A465 Heads of the Valleys road, through the Clydach Gorge and Brynmawr, turning off at the head of the Rhymney Valley.

(7) Butetown
From the rb., and A469, take B4257 to l. for Butetown. Follow this road down to its junction with A469 at Rhymney then through Bargoed and Hengoed to Ystrad Mynach. Take care at the major junction in Ystrad Mynach that you remain on the A469 for Caerphilly.

(8) Caerphilly
From Caerphilly town centre, continue on A469 for a few hundred yards, passing Cenotaph.

(9) Rudry
Turn l. into Van Road for the pleasant drive through wooded Rudry to Lower Machen. Return to Newport on A468. Visitors based in Cardiff, may return on A469 over Caerphilly Mountain.

Map labels:

Monmouth and Brecon Canal
Govilon
A4077
Llanfoist
B4246
Brynmawr
A465
6
Bute Town
7
Blaenavon
5
Rhymney
Pontlottyn
A4043
Abersychan
A469
Pontypool
Tir-phil
4
A472
Bargoed
Crumlin
Miles
Hengoed
Abercarn
0 1 2 3 4 5
Ystrad Mynach
Cwm-cam Forest Drive
0 1 2 3 4 5 6 7 8
Cross Keys
3
Kilometres
Rhymney
Ebbw
A467
Risca
Casnewydd
Newport
Llanbradach
2
8
Caerphilly
Lower Machen
A468
1
Pentre-poeth
Rudry
9

50

What to see

Newport Museum and Art Gallery

Exhibits at this museum in John Frost Square include Roman finds from Caerwent village, items relating to the archaeology and history of Gwent and sections on the Chartist movement and natural history. The Gallery has a permanent collection of paintings, and also receives regular touring exhibitions. Museum shop and information centre also on site.
Tel: Newport 840064.
Open: All year.
Multi-storey car park nearby. **F.**

Tredegar House and Country Park

near Newport

Described as 'the most splendid brick house of the 17th century in Wales', Tredegar House is set in 90 acres of parkland, now a country park. Guided tours of house. Other attractions include a boating lake, Children's Farm, donkey rides, Aquarium, Bird Garden, picnic site and adventure play area. Off M4 at Junction 28 (not on tour).
Grounds open all year. House and attractions: Summer only. **C.**

Fourteen Locks Interpretive Centre

near Newport

Before the coming of the railways, iron and coal were transported by canal from the valleys of Gwent to the docks at Newport. A section of the Monmouthshire Canal has now been restored for much of its length, providing a continuous footpath to the major feat of engineering — the Fourteen Locks, at High Cross. Here too is an Interpretive Centre, telling the story of the great Canal Age. Picnic site nearby and waymarked walks. Audio visual and teaching packs available (ideal for school visits).
Tel: Newport 894802.
Open: Easter to September.

Cwmcarn Scenic Forest Drive

This exciting 7m drive through the Ebbw Forest is a holiday must. From the high viewpoints within the coniferous forest there are exceptional views of the Bristol Channel and the Brecon Beacons.

Several picnic places are located within the forest, including an official barbecue site at Car Park 1, as well as an adventure play area for children. A series of mountain and forest walks lead off from the drive. Access from A467, south of Abercarn.
Open: Easter to August daily, 11am-8pm. September weekends only, 11am-6pm. **C.**

Pontypool Park

This pleasant park provides attractions for all the family. The fine Georgian stables now house The Valley Inheritance Pontypool, an interpretive centre where exhibitions and a film tell the story of Gwent's Eastern Valley from earliest times to the present day. A 2½ mile walk guides visitors around the features in the Park, including one of the largest artificial ski-slopes in Europe and an impressive sports and leisure complex.
Open: All year (The Valley Inheritance and Park).
Tel: Pontypool 55764 for information on leisure centre and ski-slope.

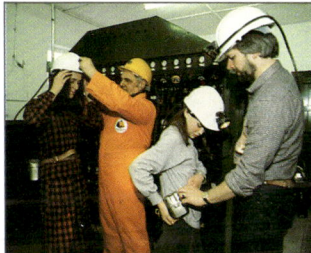
Take a trip underground at Big Pit.

Big Pit Mining Museum

Blaenavon

Big Pit was a working coalmine until 1980. Over the last few years the site has been converted into a unique visit or centre. Highlight of the visit is a conducted tour of the underground workings, during which you put on a miner's cap lamp and descend 300ft in the "pit cage". On the surface, there are fascinating exhibition areas, a blacksmith's forge, engine winding house and "Miner's Kitchen" refreshments. Blaenavon Ironworks, an important 18th century industrial site, can also be visited.
Tel: Blaenavon (0495) 790311.
Open: Spring, Summer and Autumn daily (except Mondays). Please telephone for details of Winter opening. Free car park. **C.**

Llandegfedd Reservoir and Farm Park

Though not on main tour, mention of Pontypool cannot be made without reference to the Llandegfedd Reservoir and the Farm Park. Five walks, totalling 18 miles in varied scenery of hills and woodland start from the eastern Picnic Area by the reservoir. Nearby is the Farm Park which has a collection of rare breeds of farm animals and a display of old farm implements. A pet's corner and adventure play area provided for children. Also picnic area and nature trail. Access from A472, approx. 4m north-east of Pontypool.
Tel: Farm Park — Usk 2692.
Open: Reservoir — all year. Farm Park — Easter to September. Free car park. **C.**

Butetown

near Rhymney

Butetown's unique and well planned rows of artisans' dwellings defy the conventions of the South Wales valleys' architecture. Built around 1802-3 to house the workers of the nearby ironworks, they were carefully and sympathetically restored in 1975 as part of the valley's contribution to European Architectural Heritage Year.
Open: Exteriors only, at any reasonable time. Free car park. **F.**

Caerphilly Castle

Moated Caerphilly Castle, built in the late 13th century, has the finest system of water defences in Britain. An unexpected sight is its leaning tower, which Cromwell had failed to blow up completely.
*Open: All year. Standard Hours. * Also S.M.* **C.**

Having toured Caerphilly Castle follow the recommended route to Rudry and take one of the waymarked woodland walks through Coed Coesau Whips. Alternatively take the A469 towards Cardiff, turning down a minor road to left for visit to Cefn-Onn Country Park.

TOUR 22

Rhondda, Neath & Afan Valleys

Base: *Porthcawl*

See also page 71

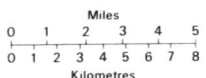

A lively family resort on the South Wales coast offering all the attractions and amenities that are part and parcel of a seaside holiday: extensive sandy beaches; a large funfair; fishing; boating; evening entertainment, and a good selection of accommodation to suit all tastes and pockets. Our short tour from Porthcawl takes you to some exciting tourist attractions which the children will enjoy, whatever the weather. *T.I.C. The Old Police Station, John Street. Tel. (065671) 6639 (E).*

(1) START: Porthcawl
From Lock's Common, follow the new road to rb. and keep straight ahead on A4106 for approx. 4m to A48. Turn rt. here for ½m, then l. at next rb.

(2) Bridgend
In town centre, take A4063 through Llangynwyd and Maesteg, joining the A4107 at Cymmer. Here turn l.

(3) Afan Argoed Country Park
From Cymmer, follow the A4107 through the thickly wooded Afan Valley to the Welsh Miners' Museum (see opp.). Return on to A4107, following road to l. to Pontrhydyfen, birthplace of Richard Burton. Turn rt. here on to B4287 for Neath.

(4) Neath
Following visit to Neath Abbey, leave town on B4434 Tonna, Resolven Road.

(5) Detour to Penscynor Wildlife Park
At Tonna, detour to rt. to A465, then to Cilfrew for visit to Wildlife Park.

(6) Vale of Neath to Hirwaun
Return to Tonna, for drive through Vale of Neath to Resolven. ½m beyond Melincourt, a footpath to

rt. leads to the 80ft high waterfalls. At Resolven, turn rt. on to A465, below the slopes of the Rheola Forest, and continue to Glyn Neath. From here drive on to. Hirwaun on alternative route.

(7) Hirwaun over Rhigos
In 4½m, approaching Hirwaun, turn rt. on to A4061 for the ascent over the Rhigos, a fine mountain road built by out-of-work miners during the 30s. Viewing point and car park on rt. at Craig y Llyn. Beyond the dizzy heights of the 1,600ft summit descend into the Rhondda towns of Treherbert and Treorchy.

(8) Treorchy over Bwlch
At Treorchy, follow A4061 mountain road to rt., as it twists its way over the 1,500ft Bwlch-y-Clawdd Pass. Continue on A4061 into the Ogmore Valley, returning to Bridgend through the villages of Blackmill and Litchard. Coity Castle is down an unclassified road to l. From Bridgend and A48 follow the signs to Porthcawl.

What to see

Welsh Miners' Museum

A museum not of mining but miners, showing the harsh realities of "coal getting" in the South Wales Valleys. See how they lived in the typical miner's cottage scene so vividly re-created here, then enter the simulated coal face to see how men, women and children worked in the mines. Other displays complete the story of coal, illustrating pit gear and mining equipment, the major tragedies in the history of the industry, the social activities of the miners, and new developments in the modern mines.
Open: Easter to October, daily. Weekends only in winter. Free car park. **C.**

Afan Argoed Country Park
Cymmer

Adjoining the Welsh Miners' Museum is a countryside centre for the Afan Argoed Country Park. Here visitors are given a greater understanding of the environment and the natural history of the forested Afan Valley. A series of easy-to-follow, waymarked walks, suitable for families, start from the centre. Longer, more demanding Forest Trails have also been designed for the more energetic and adventurous rambler. Picnic sites and refreshments cabin provided.
Open: All year. At any reasonable time, during daylight hours. Centre open Easter to October, daily. Weekends only in winter. Free car park. **F.**

Penscynor Wildlife Park
Cilfrew

Over 350 kinds of animals and birds, many roaming freely, can be seen in this wonderful wildlife park. You'll see baby chimps, exotic birds, diving sealions and cheeky macaws who love meeting people and being photographed. This large park also has an exciting Alpine Slide. Take a scenic chairlift to the mountain top and ride your own sled down a thrilling bob-sleigh track (without the snow and cold weather!). Penscynor is a real day out for all the family, a beautiful, bustling park with cafe, restaurant, adventure playground, shop and picnic sites.
Tel. Neath (0639) 2189.
Open: All year, daily, from 10am. No admittance after 6pm in main season, or dusk during Autumn to Spring. **C** *for car park.* **C.**

Neath Abbey

Abbots of Neath Abbey would have turned in their graves at the thought of their sacred site being used for industrial purposes in the 18th century. Copper was smelted in the three-bay presbytery, and later the nearby ironworks used the abbey kitchen as a foundry. Near the significant remains of the abbey are the ruins of two blast furnaces, 60-70ft high. ¾m west of Neath town centre.

Open: Standard Hours. * *Free car park.* **C.**

Coity Castle

Coity, like many of the Vale of Glamorgan castles, dates back to the days of the Norman lordships. The oldest part of the castle, the square keep, is of 12th century origin, while the rest is 14th century, when the castle was extensively rebuilt. Additions were made in Tudor times. 1m to the left off A4061, approaching Bridgend.
Open: All year. Standard Hours. *
C.

Sculpture of Aneurin Bevan at Margam Park.

Margam Country Park

Margam Park, though off the main tour, is only 20 minutes' drive from Porthcawl (along A48 and M4). Over 4,000 years history is found within Margam's 850 acres — iron age hill fort, Orangery and Castle. The landscape parkland with its famous deer herd contrasts with the Orangery's formal gardens. Facilities include the Coach House Theatre, Exhibition, Visitor Centre and activities for the children including the adventure playground. In June 1983 a major exhibition of British Sculpture opened in the grounds and features some 66 works of art.
Open: Park — all year, dawn to dusk. Orangery — Easter to October. **F. C** *for Orangery.*

Further attractions

Aberdulais Falls (N.T.)
Summer shows: Grand Pavilion, Porthcawl.
Theatre: Berwyn Centre, Nantymoel.
Museum: John Street, Porthcawl.
Walks: Coed Morgannwg Way from the Rhigos to Margam Park. Also in Rhondda Forest, starting from forest entrance on A4061 Hirwaun to Treorchy road (signposted).

Gower Peninsula

Base: *Swansea*

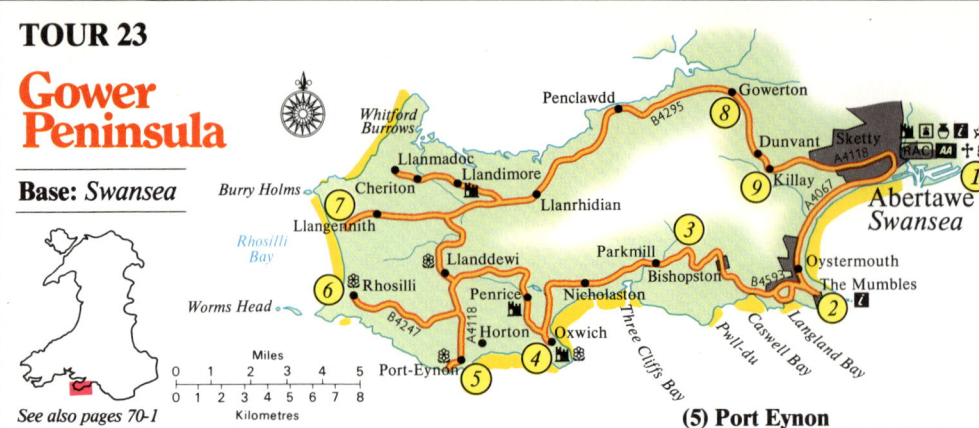

See also pages 70-1

Wales's second largest city is just on the doorstep of 'an area of outstanding natural beauty', the Gower Peninsula. Modern Swansea has some spacious and attractive hotels, a lively nightlife with plenty of pubs, clubs, theatres and cinemas, excellent shopping facilities, museums, an art gallery and a super leisure centre. *T.I.C. Crymlyn Burrows, Jersey Marine. Tel. (0792) 462403 (E). Also Civic Information Centre, PO Box 59, Singleton Street, Swansea SA1 3QG. Tel. (0792) 468321 (1-12).*

(1) START: Swansea
Follow A4067 from city centre, passing the new leisure centre and museum on sea front. S/P Mumbles and Gower.

Swansea's exciting leisure centre.

(2) Oystermouth
In 1½m arrive in Oystermouth, turning rt. uphill on B4593 S/P Langland Bay/Caswell. Follow signs for Langland Bay, descending a steep hill to the sandy beach (car park, quiet headland walks). Proceed up Brynfield Road from car park for Caswell Bay.

(3) Bishopston
From Caswell, follow road to rt. to T junction, turning l. for Bishopston. After 1¼m turn l. on to B4436, through Kittle, and in ½m turn rt. In ¾m turn on to A4118 S/P Parkmill, Port Eynon.

(4) Oxwich
Continue on this road A4118, turning l. by ruined Penrice Castle entrance for Oxwich, passing part of the 540 acre national nature reserve (sandy beach, car park nearby).

(5) Port Eynon
Return to the A4118 via Penrice, avoiding narrow roads and turn l. for Port Eynon (sandy beach, walks). Returning to tour, follow A4118 back to Scurlage, turning l. on to B4247 for Rhosili.

(6) Rhosili
From this village renowned for its hang-gliding, as well as its extensive sandy beach and grassy headlands (car park), return to Scurlage, and turn l. on to A4118 S/P Llanddewi/Bury.

Worm's Head, near Rhosili, on the Gower Peninsula.

(7) Llangennith
At T junction with B4295, turn l. for Llangennith (sandy beach), on to the rt. detouring to Cheriton and Llanmadoc. Continue now on B4295 through Llanrhidian to Penclawdd.

(8) Gowerton
Here turn rt. on to B4296 S/P Swansea.

(9) Killay to Swansea
Beyond Dunvant, on descending hill to main junction, follow road to l. into Swansea suburbs. From Killay, keep on A4118 through Sketty to city centre.

TOUR 24

Vale of Glamorgan

Base: *Cardiff*

See also pages 71-2

Cardiff has all the amenities expected of a modern capital — hotels, restaurants, theatres and shops. That's not all. There are acres of parkland, a city-centre castle, museums, an elegant civic centre and just half an hour's drive away, the peaceful Vale of Glamorgan.

T.I.C. 3 Castle Street. Tel. (0222) 27281 (1-12).

Miles
0 1 2 3 4 5
0 1 2 3 4 5 6 7 8
Kilometres

Ogmore · Corntown · Ewenny · Ogmore · Ogmore-by-sea · Southerndown · Wick · Broughton · Monknash · Llantwit Major · St. Donat's · Boverton · St. Athan · Aberthaw · Rhoose · Porthkerry · The Knap · Barry Island · Barry · Bonvilston · St. Nicholas · Cowbridge · St. Fagans · Welsh Folk Museum · Caerdydd Cardiff

(1) START: Cardiff
Passing Castle and Centre Hotel, turn rt. at traffic lights, into Cathedral Road. Keep in l. lane as you approach the hill junction by traffic lights. Keep forward at next two junctions for St. Fagan's.

(2) St. Fagan's
Following visit to Folk Museum, turn rt. across level crossing, and follow narrow road to rb. Keep on road ahead, turn rt. at T junction, then follow A48 (S/P Port Talbot) at major rb.

(3) St. Nicholas
In 2m by traffic lights, turn l. for the splendid Dyffryn Gardens and Tinkinswood Burial Chamber. Return to A48, turning l. for Cowbridge.

(4) Cowbridge
As you approach this vale town, bear l. on to A4222, driving down 1 in 12 hill for town centre. Return to A48 again for approx. 3¾m, bearing l. for Ewenny on B4524 (Priory is on rt.). At T junction turn l., then rt. in few hundred yards on B4524. S/P Ogmore-by-Sea.

(5) Ogmore-by-Sea
Note the ruins of 12th century castle as you follow the Ogmore river to the sea. Follow coast road up hill, through Southerndown (sandy beach) to join B4265 at St. Brides Major. Turn rt. here, detouring to l. in approx. 2m for villages of Broughton, Monknash, Marcross and St. Donat's.

(6) Llantwit Major
Beyond St. Donat's drive downhill into Llantwit Major, and from the quaint square take road to rt. S/P Barry. Proceed on this road to join fast new road to rt. S/P Barry.

(7) Porthkerry and Barry
Following the signs for Barry, turn rt. at second rb. and keep forward, at all crossroads, to Barry Island whose major attraction is an amazing Pleasure Park with holiday entertainment for all the family. Porthkerry Country Park is off this road (A4050) to the rt. Return to Cardiff on the direct A4055 'top' road, or take the alternative coastal route through Sully and Penarth.

A children's paradise, Barry Island's Pleasure Park.

Attractions at a glance
Aberthaw: power station; pottery.
Barry Island: beaches; pleasure park; pottery.
St. Nicholas: Dyffryn Gardens; Tinkinswood Burial Chamber.
Cowbridge: Old Hall exhibitions; pottery; shops.
Ewenny: priory; potteries.
Llantwit Major: 6th century church; museum; pebble beach.
Ogmore-by-Sea: beach; castle.
Penarth: Turner House Art Gallery; beach.
St. Donat's: arts centre.
St. Fagan's: Welsh Folk Museum.

Cardiff, the capital

Roath Park and Lake

Welsh Folk Museum, St Fagan's

Llandaf Cathedral

National Museum and Civic Centre

Cardiff Castle

Welsh Industrial and Maritime Museum

Cardiff, the capital of Wales, can be explored on foot, by bus or in the comfort of your own car. In the summer months tours are arranged by open-top buses (weather permitting) to many of the city's attractions, including Llandaff Cathedral and the Industrial and Maritime Museum. Timetables are available from the information centre in Castle Street.

Cardiff Castle

A splendid city-centre castle with 1,900 years of history, restored in the Victorian era, with opulent state rooms depicting a variety of scenes from Greek Mythology, the Bible and the Canterbury Tales. The restoration was by architect William Burges, who also designed Castell Coch, at nearby Tongwynlais.

Visitors to Cardiff Castle can see Roman Walls, a Norman Keep, mediaeval towers and the Welch Regiment Museum. Guided tours, mediaeval banquets and Welsh lunches are also held here.
Tel: (0222) 31279 (Castle enquiries). 372737 (Banquets). Open: All year. Times shown at main entrance. **C.**

Llandaff Cathedral

Established in the 6th century by St. Seiriol, this fine cathedral in the village of Llandaff, has been renewed and restored over the centuries to its present splendour.

Epstein's 'Christ in Majesty' sculpture dominates the splendid interior. Nearby are the ruins of the Bishop's Palace.

Welsh Folk Museum

St. Fagan's

Within the walls of a Norman castle, there is an Elizabethan mansion house recently restored. The picturesque parkland contains a superb collection of traditional buildings brought from all parts of Wales and re-erected stone by stone. They include furnished cottages and farmhouses, a working woollen mill and corn mill, a barn, tannery, smithy, chapel, tollhouse and cockpit. In addition, there are indoor galleries illustrating domestic, social and cultural life in Wales, farming techniques and fishing. Cafe, restaurant, shop. Car park.
Open: All year. **C.**

National Museum of Wales

The story of Wales from earliest times, including its geological and zoological history, its archaeology, art and industry, is told by means of exhibits and lively newly-designed galleries. There's even a simulated coalmine, right here in the civic centre. In addition, the National Museum has a remarkable collection of modern European painting and sculpture. There are changing exhibitions too, with a new one opening on average every fortnight.

Holiday activities arranged for children. Also lunchtime concerts, readings, lectures and other events. Restaurant, bookshop.
Open: All year. Weekdays 10am-5pm. Sun 2.30-5.00pm. Closed Christmas, Boxing Day, New Year's Day, Good Friday and May Day. **F.**

Welsh Industrial and Maritime Museum

Appropriately located in Cardiff's dockland is this most recent addition to the city's range of attractions. Exhibits include a number of pumping, winding and driving engines, all restored to working order. Many large outdoor exhibits are also on display, including a pilot cutter, canal boat, cranes, an industrial locomotive and a full-size working replica of Trevithick's pioneering steam locomotive.
Open: Same hours as National Museum. **F.**

Across Wales

Our map opposite shows some suggested tour routes across Wales, ideal for those wishing to make a week of touring. From the main route you can detour on one or more of the shorter tours featured in this guide, to make a holiday journey to suit your own particular needs. Finding places to stay en route should be easy if you take advantage of the bed booking service operated at Tourist Information Centres throughout Wales (see page 9).

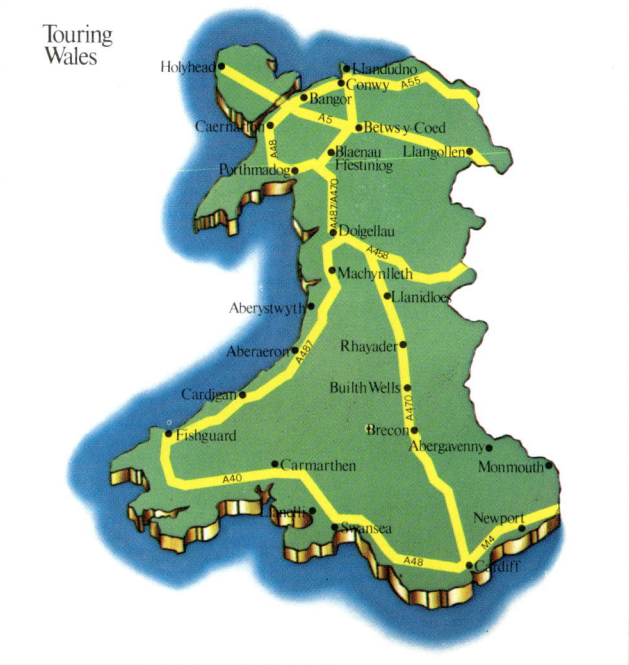

Touring Wales

Tour 1
Cardiff to Conwy

The north-south A470 takes in some of the finest scenery in Wales. The Brecon Beacons National Park, the Cambrian Mountains, the Cader Idris range, the Snowdonia National Park and the beautiful vales of Lledr and Conwy are all on this easy to follow route. The detailed road maps at the back of the book show many of the holiday attractions to be seen on the way.

Pen-y-fan, the 2,907ft peak of the Brecon Beacons.

Tour 2
The West Coast

There's no easier way to tour the western coast of Wales, from Porthmadog in the north to St. David's in the south, than to follow the A487.
This is a fast, but convenient route, giving access to much of the Pembrokeshire Coast, to resorts such as Aberaeron, Aberystwyth and New Quay on the Cardigan Coast, Porthmadog and Caernarfon.

New Quay, on the Cardigan Coast.

Tour 3
Telford's Route

The A5 is a fast route into North Wales from the Midlands and the south-east. Being a former coaching route built by Thomas Telford in the early 19th century, there are lots of cosy old inns along this road — in attractive market towns and mountain villages. Branching off from this main route is a network of good scenic roads into Snowdonia and the moorlands and lakelands of North Wales. From Llangollen, Betws-y-Coed or even Corwen you could join one of the illustrated tours in this guide, including the Snowdon Tour (page 14) and the Lakelands Tour (page 20).

Cruising along the Llangollen canal.

Coming from Abroad

It's so easy travelling around Wales. Even the overseas visitor, unfamiliar with driving on the left, will soon get accustomed to the relatively quiet, traffic-free roads of Wales. To help you on your way, we have included here some useful facts and figures to make your tour of Wales as enjoyable as possible.

Legend:
- ▬ Motorways
- ▬ Main roads
- ✈ Airports

ROAD ROUTES INTO WALES
From main airports & seaports

Getting to Wales

From the map opposite you'll see that Wales is easily accessible from the main entry points into Britain. For those in a hurry, the fastest, most convenient route into South Wales is the M4 motorway, now extended further west, making Pembrokeshire that much nearer in terms of travelling time. The A40 provides a scenic alternative from the south-east. Access into Mid Wales is also easy, from the main U.K. motorway network. Overseas motorists normally enter North Wales on one of two main routes, the A5 London — Holyhead trunk road, or the A55 coast road from Chester, linked to the main motorway by the M56.

Motoring Organisations

If you are a member of a motoring organisation in your own country, you should enquire whether it has reciprocal arrangements with the Automobile Association (AA) in Britain. Alternatively you can join as an overseas member either the AA (Fanum House, Basingstoke, Hants RG21 2EA) or the Royal Automobile Club (83-85 Pall Mall, London SW1), both of which offer a comprehensive service for motorists in all parts of Britain. These organisations will come to your assistance in the event of a breakdown. If you get into difficulties on a quiet country road, phone the local telephone exchange (dial 100) and you will get the number of the nearest AA or RAC office.

Rules of the Road

Traffic in Wales, as in the rest of Britain, keeps to the left and at traffic islands or roundabouts gives way to vehicles approaching from the right. Motorists always overtake on the right. On narrow single-track country lanes, always use the nearest, most convenient passing place, giving priority to vehicles going uphill. Thousands of visitors from overseas come to Wales every year, and have no difficulties at all in adjusting to motoring on the left or driving on some of the 'off-the-beaten' track routes.

Speed Limits

Distances and speed limits on road signs are given in miles.

(1 mile = 1.6km). The maximum speed limits on motorways in Britain are 70 miles per hour (113 kilometres per hour) and also on roads with dual carriageways. On other roads the limit is 60 miles per hour. In built up areas, towns and villages, lower limits apply (usually 30 or 40 mph), as indicated on the road signs.

Road Signs

In Wales, on our main roads in particular, place names on road signs may appear in both English and Welsh. For example, Swansea and Abertawe, Carmarthen and Caerfyrddin. The English spelling always

Visitors from abroad will have no difficulty touring Wales, which is only about 200 miles from north to south. Finding accommodation won't be difficult either, if you make use of the network of tourist information centres.

Distances to Wales from main ports of entry
(approximate)

	miles	(kms)
Dover	211	(350)
Felixstowe	212	(351)
Folkestone	203	(338)
Harwich	202	(337)
Hull	134	(223)
Liverpool	20	(33)
London-Tilbury	116	(276)
Newhaven	158	(263)
Ramsgate	211	(350)
Southampton	89	(148)
Weymouth	95	(152)

Distances
Miles and Kilometres
All distances in this guide are calculated in miles. The following table will help you quickly convert the mileages quoted.

Miles	Miles Kms	Kms
0.62	1	1.61
1.24	2	3.22
1.86	3	4.83
2.48	4	6.44
3.11	5	8.05
3.78	6	9.66
4.35	7	11.27
4.97	8	12.87
5.59	9	14.48
6.20	10	16.10
12.40	20	32.20
18.60	30	48.30
24.80	40	64.40
31.00	50	80.50
37.00	60	96.60
43.00	70	112.70
50.00	80	128.70
56.00	90	144.80
62.00	100	161.00

To quickly convert miles to kms, multiply the number of miles by 8 and divide the result by 5.

appears above the Welsh. To help you get familiarized with the place names, we have, wherever possible, included both the English and Welsh equivalents on the maps at the back of this guide, as they appear on the road signs.

Car Hire

If you are not bringing your own car on holiday, many of the leading car hire firms in Britain, such as Avis, Hertz and Godfrey Davis, will arrange for a car to meet you at your ferry port or airport of arrival. And under the 'one-way hiring system' operated by the larger companies, you don't have to return the car to the original pick-up point. This gives you greater freedom to go where you please, without the hassle of keeping to a rigid pre-planned route.
Details of car hire facilities in Britain are obtainable from your local travel agent or from your British Tourist Authority office.

Petrol

In Britain, petrol is graded by a star system ranging from the low quality two-star (90 octanes minimum) to the high compression quality four star (97 octanes minimum). Petrol stations in Wales invariably sell two, three and four star petrol; many also sell diesel fuel. On main roads you'll find plenty of petrol stations, but on the remoter mountain roads, make sure you have a full tank before you set off. 24-hour petrol stations can be found in towns and cities, and on certain busy main roads.

Banking Hours
Foreign currency and travellers cheques may be exchanged at any bank in Wales during normal banking hours, which are Monday to Friday, 9.30am-3.30pm. Certain travel agents and hotels also have money changing facilities.

Tyre pressures

Kg/ Sq cm	lb/ sq in	Kg/ sq cm	lb/ sq in
1.62	23	1.83	26
1.69	24	1.90	27
1.76	25	1.97	28

Overseas Offices

To help you plan your visit to Britain, the British Tourist Authority has a network of overseas offices, providing information about all aspects of holidays in Britain, including route maps and accommodation guides.

AUSTRALIA
British Tourist Authority,
171 Clarence Street, Sydney,
N.S.W. 2000. T. 29-8627
AUSTRIA
British Tourist Authority,
Wiedner Hauptstrasse 5/8,
.1040 Wien. T. (0222) 65 03 76
BELGIUM
British Tourist Authority,
Rue de la Montagne 52 Bergstraat,
B2 1000 Brussels. T. 02/511.43.90
BRAZIL
British Tourist Authority,
Avenida Ipiranga 318-A,
12° Andar, conj 1201 01046 Sao
Paulo = SP. T. 257-1834
CANADA
British Tourist Authority,
94 Cumberland Street,
Suite 600, Toronto, Ontario
M5R 3N3. T. (416) 925-6326
DENMARK
Det Britiske Turistkontor,
Montergade 3, DK-1116
Kobenhavn. T. (01) 12 07 93
FRANCE
British Tourist Authority,
6 Place Vendôme, 75001 Paris.
T. 296 47 60
GERMANY
British Tourist Authority,
Neue Mainzer Str. 22, 6000
Frankfurt am Main 1.
T. (0611) 23 64 28/29
ITALY
British Tourist Authority,
Via S. Eufemia 5,
00187 Rome.
T. 678.4998 or 678.5548
JAPAN
British Tourist Authority,
Tokyo Club Building, 3-2-6
Kasumigaseki, Chiyoda-ku,
Tokyo 100. T. (03) 581-3603
MEXICO
British Tourist Authority,
Rio Tiber 103-6 piso, Mexico
5 DF, 06500.
T. 511.39.27 or 514.93.56
NETHERLANDS
British Tourist Authority
(Written enquiries only),
Leidseplein, 5 1017 PR
Amsterdam. T. (020) 23.46.67
British Travel Centre
(Personal callers only)

Leidseplein 23, Amsterdam.
NEW ZEALAND
British Tourist Authority,
Box 3655, Wellington.
NORWAY
British Tourist Authority,
Mariboes gt 11, Oslo 1.
T. (02) 41 18 49
SINGAPORE
British Tourist Authority,
Room 403,
Singapore Rubber House,
14 Collyer Quay, Singapore 0104.
T. Singapore 2242966/7
SOUTH AFRICA
British Tourist Authority,
7th Floor, JBS Building,
107 Commissioner Street,
Johannesburg 2001,
PO Box 6256. T. (010 27 11) 29
6770
SPAIN
British Tourist Authority,
Torre de Madrid 6/4,
Plaza de Espana, Madrid 13,
Espana. T. 241 13 96
SWEDEN
British Tourist Authority
For visitors: Malmskillnadsg 42

1st Floor.
For Mail: Box 7293, S-103 90
Stockholm. T. 08-21 24 44
SWITZERLAND
British Tourist Authority,
Limmatquai 78, 8001 Zurich.
T. 01/47 42 77 or 47 42 97
USA CHICAGO
British Tourist Authority,
John Hancock Center Suite 3320,
875 N. Michigan Avenue, Chicago,
Illinois 60611.
USA DALLAS
British Tourist Authority,
Plaza of the Americas,
750 North Tower LB346,
Dallas, Texas 75201.
T. (214) 748-2279
USA LOS ANGELES
British Tourist Authority,
612 South Flower Street,
Los Angeles, CA 90017.
T. (213) 623-8196
USA NEW YORK
British Tourist Authority,
680 Fifth Avenue,
New York, NY10019.
T. (212) 581-4700

Wales in maps

On the following pages we have included a series of more detailed 5 miles to the inch road maps covering the whole of Wales. These are designed to help you get out and about in Wales. They are also keyed in to the tour maps in the main part of the book, showing you the location of tour bases and attractions of interest in relation to *your* holiday area. With the aid of these maps you can tailor the suggested tours to your own particular needs.

Key to Symbols

✈ Airport or Airfield

🏛 Building of historic association or architectural interest

🏰 Castle or defensive works

✝ Cathedral, abbey, priory or notable Christian site

🏰 Country Park

⛪ Early Christian monument

🚶 Walk: Nature Trails, Forest Trails, Long distance walks, Town Trails, and Heritage Trails

⚱ Prehistoric site of importance

▪ Roman site

🛥 Sea Fishing boats

🏄 Surfing beach

ℹ Tourist Information Centre

🤿 Underwater swimming facilities

🎿 Water Skiing

⛵ Yacht or boat club

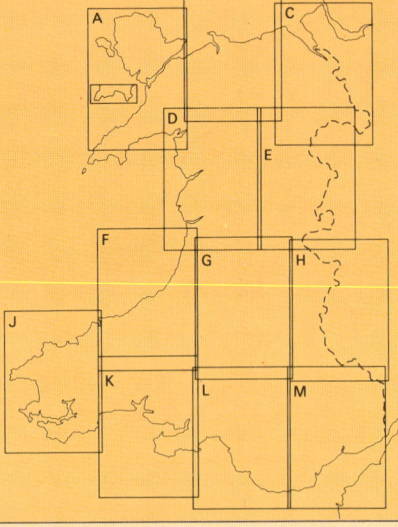

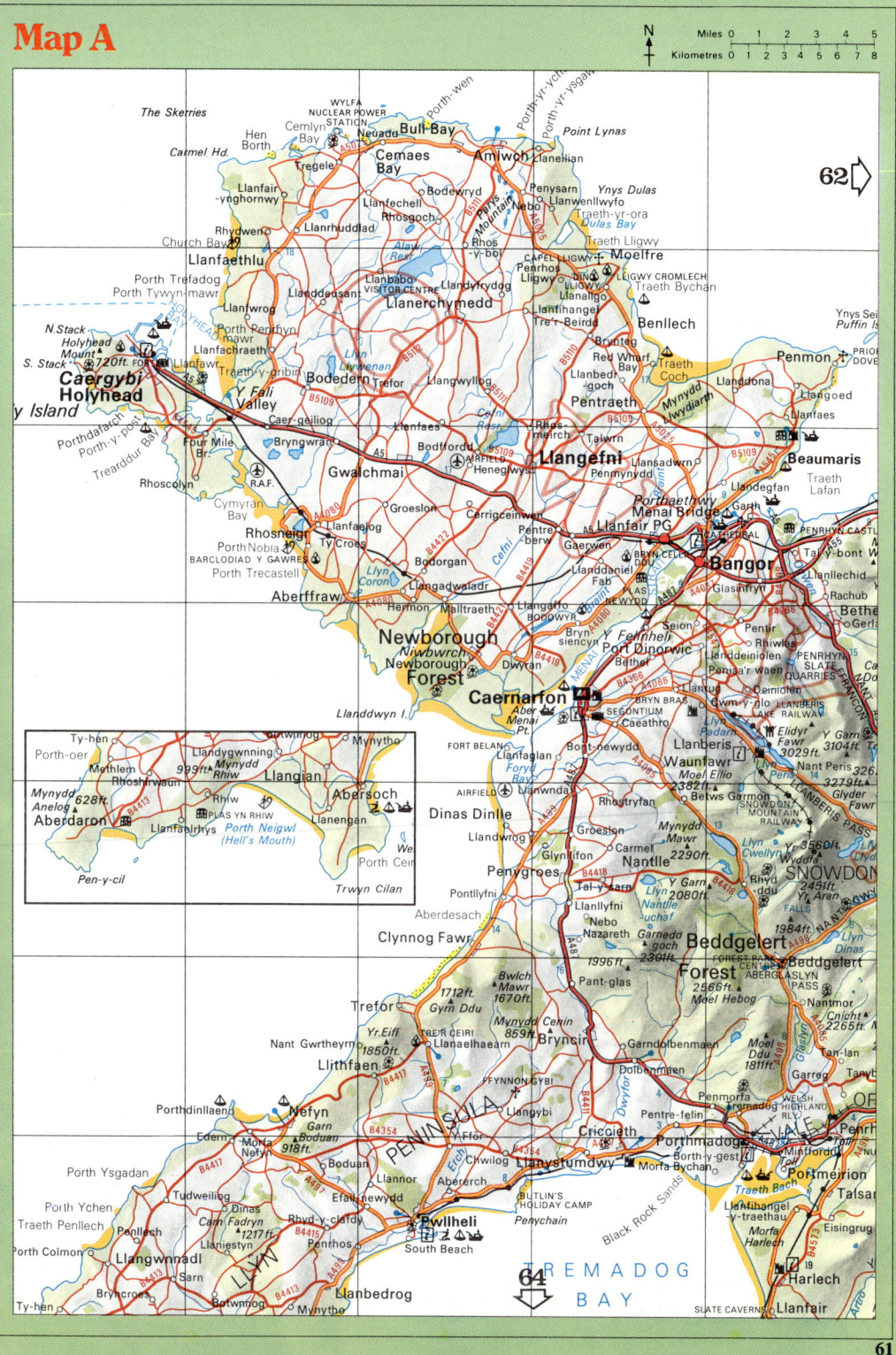

N

| Miles | 0 | 1 | 2 | 3 | 4 | 5 |
| Kilometres | 0 | 1 | 2 | 3 | 4 | 5 | 6 | 7 | 8 |

62 ⇨

The Skerries

WYLFA
NUCLEAR POWER
STATION
Porth-wen
Porth-yr-ychan

Cemlyn
Bay
Hen
Borth
Neuadd
Bull Bay
Point Lynas
Carmel Hd.
Tregele
Cemaes
Bay
Amlwch
Llaneilian
Ynys Dulas

Llanfair
-ynghornwy
Bodewryd
Llanfechell
Rhosgoch
Penysarn
Nebo
Llanwenllwyfo
Traeth-yr-ora
Dulas Bay

Rhydwen
Llanrhuddlad
Bryn
Mountain
Rhos
-y-bol
Capel Lligwy
Penrhos
Lligwy
Traeth Lligwy
Moelfre

Church Bay
Llanddeusant
LLanbabo
VISITOR CENTRE
Llandyfrydog
Dina'
Lligwy
LLIGWY CROMLECH
Traeth Bychan

Llanfaethlu
Porth Trefadog
Porth Tywyn-mawr
Llanerchymedd
Llanfihangel
Tre'r Beirdd
Benllech

Llanfwrog
Alaw
Res
Brynteg
Red Wharf
Bay
Traeth
Coch
Penmon
PRIORY
DOVE

Porth Penrhyn
Porth Penrhyn
mawr
Llyn
Alaw
Llanwyllog
Llanbedr
-goch
Mynydd
Llwydiarth
Llanddona

N.Stack
Holyhead
Mount
S. Stack
Caergybi
Holyhead
y Island
720ft. FORT
Llanfwrog
Traeth-y-gribin
Y Fali
Valley
Trefor
B5110
Pentraeth
Llanfaes
Llangoed
Beaumaris

Porthdafarch
Porth-y-post
Caer-geiliog
Rhosmeirch
Talwrn
Llansadwrn
Traeth
Lafan

Trearddur Bay
Four Mile
Br.
Bryngwran
Bodffordd
AIRFIELD
Heneglwys
Llangefni
Penmynydd
Llandegfan

Rhoscolyn
R.A.F.
Gwalchmai
B5109

Cymyran
Bay
Groeslon
Cerrigceinwen
Pentre
berw
Porthaethwy
Menai Bridge
Garth
PENRHYN CASTLE

Rhosneigr
Llanfaelog
Ty Croes
Gaerwen
Llanfair PG
Bryn Celli
Bangor
Tal-y-bont
W

Porth Nobla
BARCLODIAD Y GAWRES
Porth Trecastell
Bodorgan
Llanddaniel
Fab
PLAS
NEWYDD
BODOWYR
Seion
Glasinfryn
Rachub
Bethe
Gerl

Aberffraw
Llyn
Coron
Llangadwaladr
Hermon
Malltraeth
Llangaffo
Bryn
siencyn
Pentir
Rhiwlas
PENRHYN
SLATE
QUARRIES

Newborough
Niwbwrch
Newborough
FOREST
Dwyran
B4419
Felinheli
Port Dinorwic
Bethel
Llandeiniolen
Penisa'r waen
Deiniolen

Caernarfon
Aber
Menai
Pt.
Bryn Bras
SEGONTIUM
Caeathro
Llanrug
Cwm-y-glo
LLANBERIS
LAKE RAILWAY
Gwm

Llanddwyn I.
FORT BELAN
Llanfaglan
Foryd
Bay
Bont-newydd
Llanberis
Waunfawr
Moel Eilio
2382ft.
Elidir
Fawr
3029ft.
Y Garn
3104ft.
Nant Peris
326.
SNOWDON
MOUNTAIN
RAILWAY

Ty-hen
Porth-oer
Mynytho
AIRFIELD
Llanwnda
Rhostryfan
Betws Garmon
SNOWDON
3560ft.
Glyder
Fawr

Mynydd
Rhiw
999ft.
Llandygwnning
Rhoshirwaun
Llangian
Abersoch
Dinas Dinlle
Llandwrog
Groeslon
Carmel
Mynydd
Mawr
2290ft.
Rhyd
ddu
3279ft.
Llyn
Cwellyn
FALLS
2451ft.
Y Aran
SNOWDON

Mynydd
Anelog
628ft.
Aberdaron
PLAS YN RHIW
Llanfaelrhys
Llanengan
Porth Neigwl
(Hell's Mouth)
Penygroes
Nantlle
Llanllyfni
Tal-y-sarn
Y Garn
2080ft.
Nantlle
uchaf
Garnedd
goch
2301ft.
1984ft.
Llyn
Dinas
Beddgelert
Forest

Pen-y-cil
Porth Cei
Trwyn Cilan
Aberdesach
Nebo
Nazareth
1996ft.
Pant-glas
2566ft.
Moel Hebog
Beddgelert
FOREST PARK
ABERGLASLYN
PASS
Nantmor
Cnicht
2265ft.

Clynnog Fawr
A499
Bwlch
Mawr
1670ft.
Mynydd
Cenin
859ft.
Bryncir
Garndolbenmaen
Moel
Ddu
1811ft.
Tan-lan
Garreg
Tanybw

Trefor
Yr Eifl
1712ft.
Gyrn Ddu
TRE'R CEIRI
1850ft.
Llanaelhaearn
Dolbenmaen
Penmorfa
WELSH
HIGHLAND
RLY.
OF

Nant Gwrtheyrn
Garn
Boduan
918ft.
FFYNNON GYBI
Llangybi
Dwyfor
Pentre-felin
Tremadog
Tremadog
Porthmadog
Minffordd
Portmeirion
Talsar

Llithfaen
Nefyn
Boduan
Criccieth
Llanystumdwy
Porthmadog
Borth-y-gest
Porthmadog

Porthdinllaen
Edern
Morfa
Nefyn
Y Ffor
Chwilog
Erch
B4354
Llanystumdwy
Morfa Bychan
Eisingrug
Llanfihangel
-y-traethau
Morfa
Harlech
Harlech

Porth Ysgadan
Tudweiliog
Dinas
Cam Fadryn
1217ft.
Boduan
Llannor
Abererch
BUTLIN'S
HOLIDAY CAMP
Penychain
Black Rock Sands
Traeth Bach
19

Porth Ychen
Traeth Penllech
Porth Colmon
Penllech
Brynhcroes
Rhyd-y-clafdy
Penthos
Pwllheli
South Beach
Llanbedrog
TREMADOG
BAY
SLATE CAVERNS
Llanfair

Llangwnnadl
Sarn
Botwnnog
Mynytho
64 ⇩
LLYN
PENINSULA

Ty-hen

61

Map B

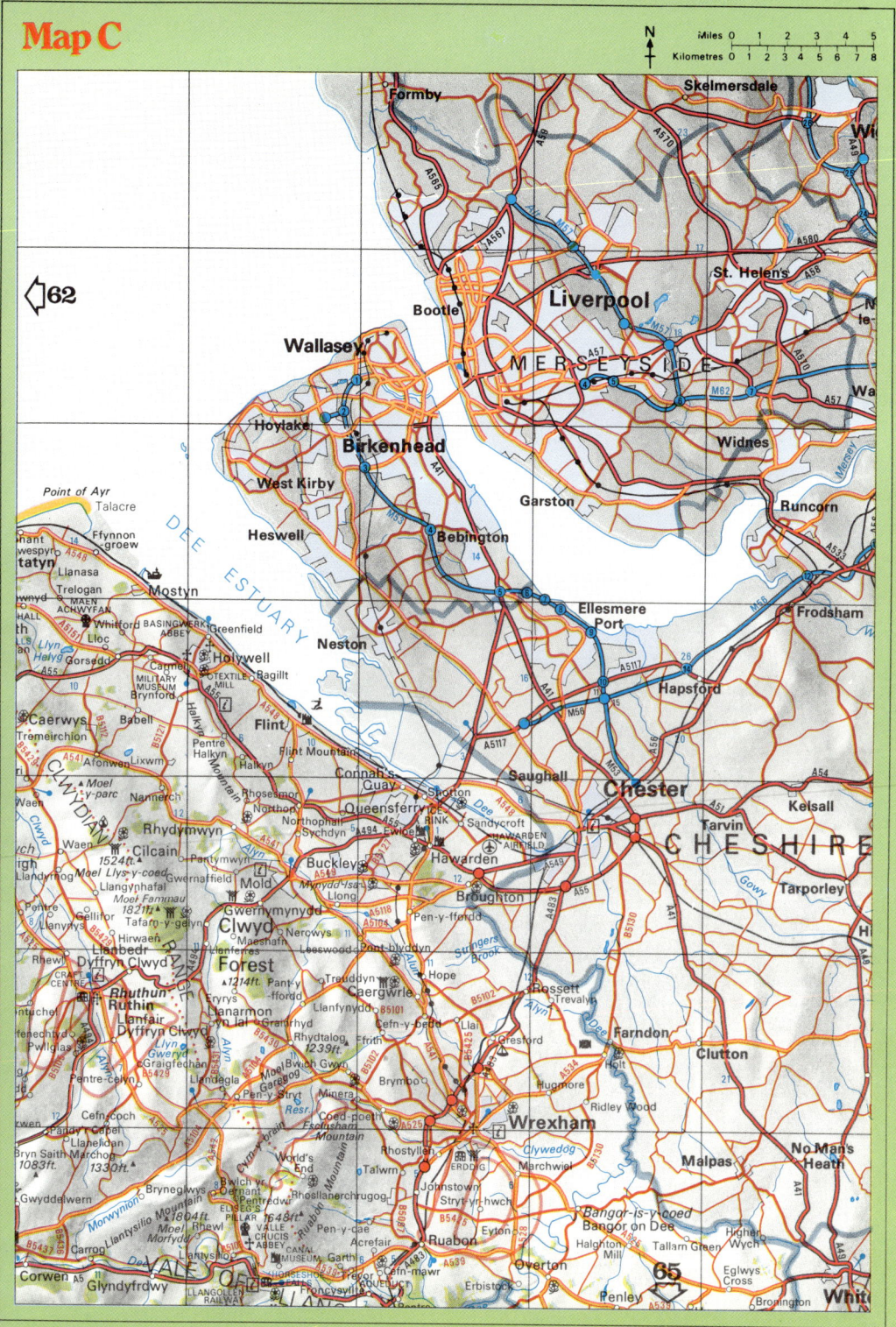

Map C

◁62

Formby
Skelmersdale
Wi
St. Helen's
Liverpool
Bootle
MERSEYSIDE
Wallasey
Wa
Hoylake
Birkenhead
Widnes
West Kirby
Garston
Runcorn
Heswell
Point of Ayr
Talacre
DEE ESTUARY
Bebington
Mostyn
Ellesmere Port
Frodsham
Ffynnon-groew
Llanasa
Trelogan
Greenfield
Neston
Hapsford
Whitford
BASINGWERK ABBEY
MAEN ACHWYFAN
Holywell
Gorsedd
Caerwys
Tremeirchion
TEXTILE MILL
Bagillt
Flint
Pentre Halkyn
Halkyn
Halkyn Mountain
Saughall
Chester
Kelsall
Moel-y-parc
Nannerch
Rhosesmor
Northop
Connah's Quay
Flint Mountain
Tarvin
Rhydymwyn
Cilcain
Pantymwyn
Queensferry
Ewloe
HAWARDEN AIRFIELD
CHESHIRE
Tarporley
Buckley
Hawarden
Llandyrnog
Llanynys
Gwernaffield
Mold
Llong
Broughton
Gwernymynydd
Clwyd
Nercwys
Pen-y-ffordd
Forest
Maeshafn
Leeswood
Pont-blyddyn
Sungers Brook
Llanbedr
Dyffryn Clwyd
Treuddyn
Hope
Rossett
Trevalyn
Farndon
Rhuthun
Ruthin
Eryrys
Llanarmon-yn-Ial
Nerquis
Gresford
Clutton
Llanfair
Dyffryn Clwyd
Graigfechan
Llandegla
Ffrith
Llanfynydd
Cefn-y-bedd
Llai
Holt
Cefn-coch
Minera
Brymbo
Hugmore
Ridley Wood
Coed-poeth
Frohisham Mountain
Wrexham
No Man's Heath
Rhostyllen
Clywedog
Marchwiel
Malpas
World's End
Talwrn
Johnstown
Rhoslanerchrugog
Bangor-is-y-coed
Bangor on Dee
Higher Wych
Ruabon
Eyton
Overton
Penley
Corwen
Glyndyfrdwy
Llangollen
Bangor on Dee
Eglwys Cross
Bromington
White

65◁

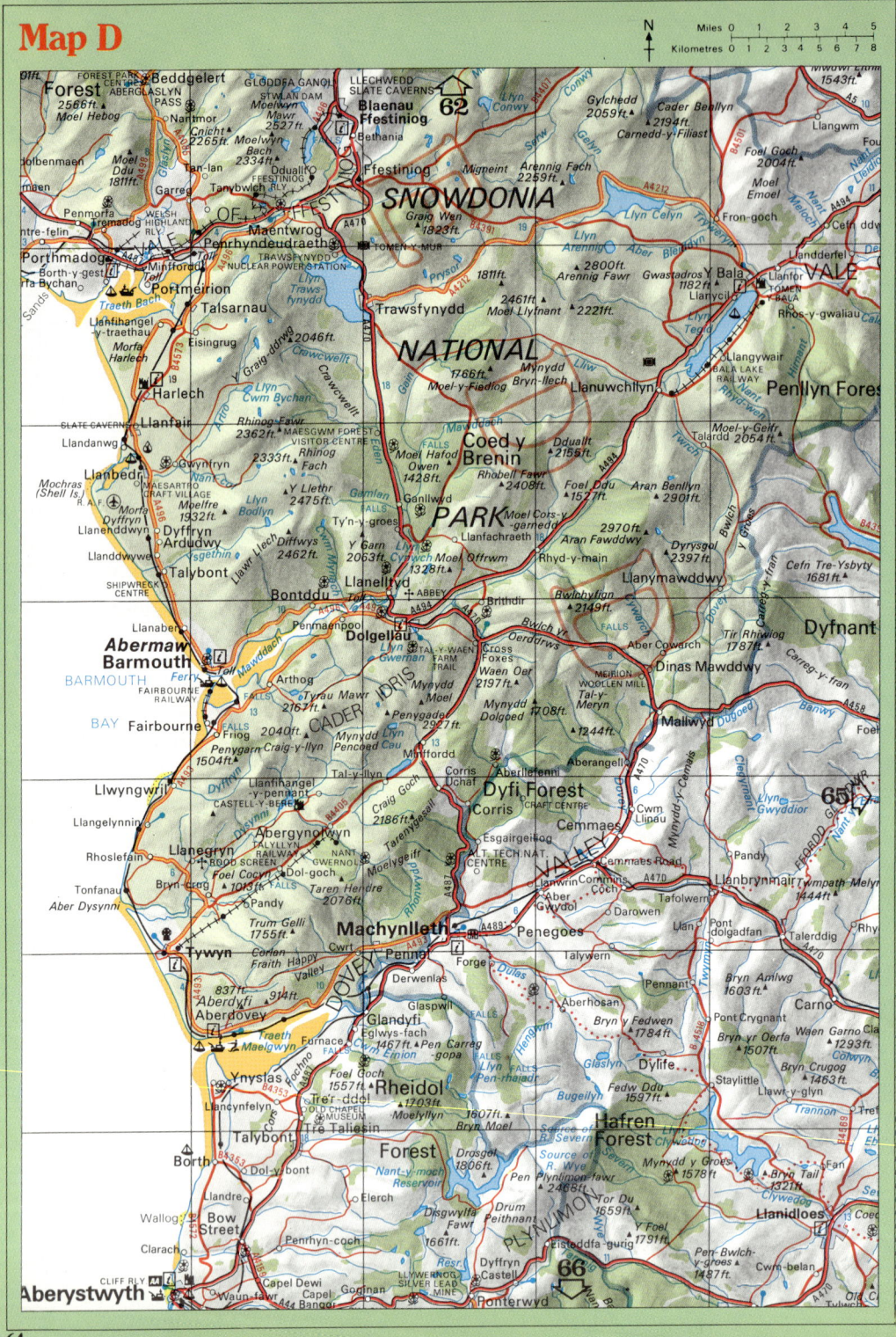

Map D

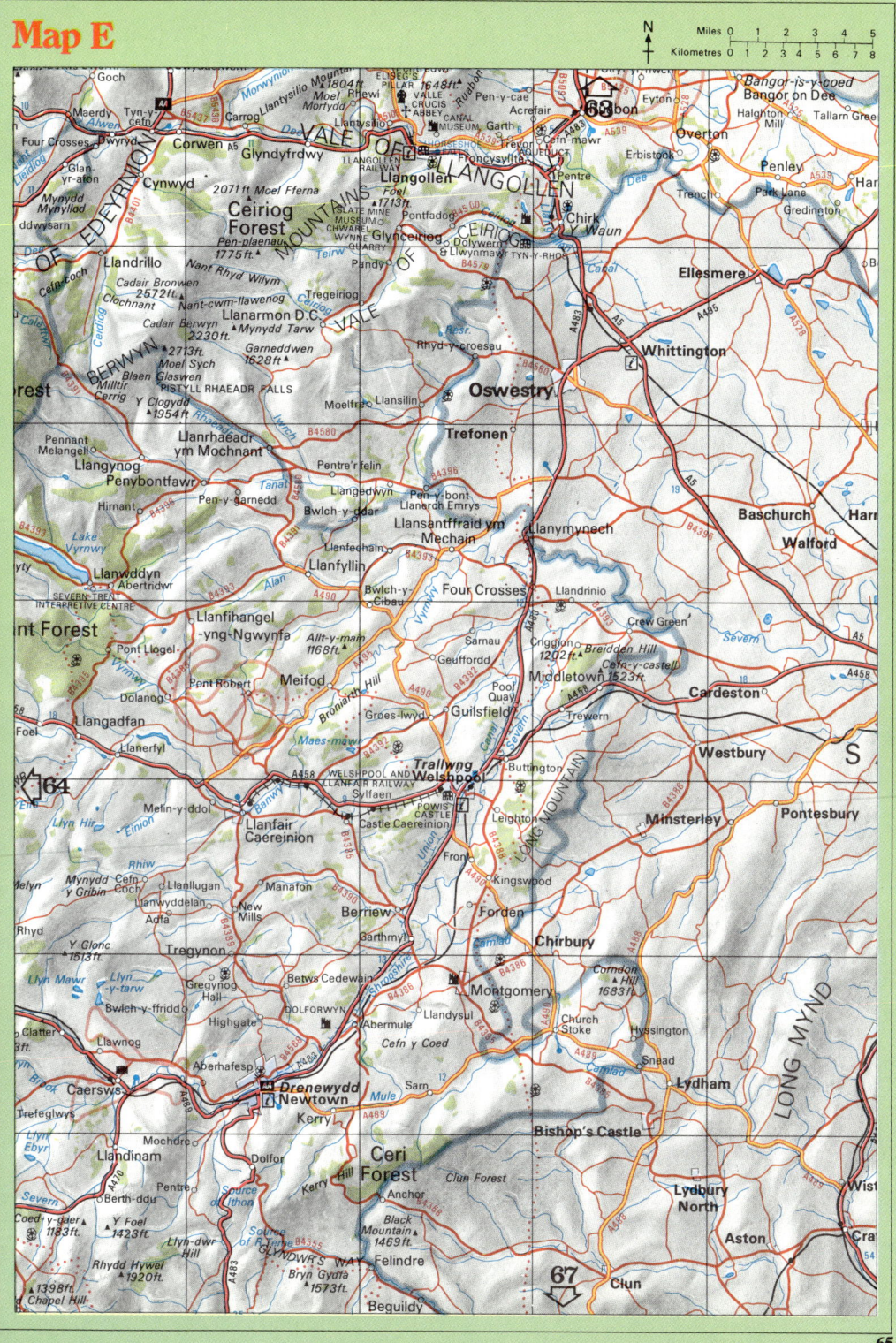

N

Miles 0 1 2 3 4 5
Kilometres 0 1 2 3 4 5 6 7 8

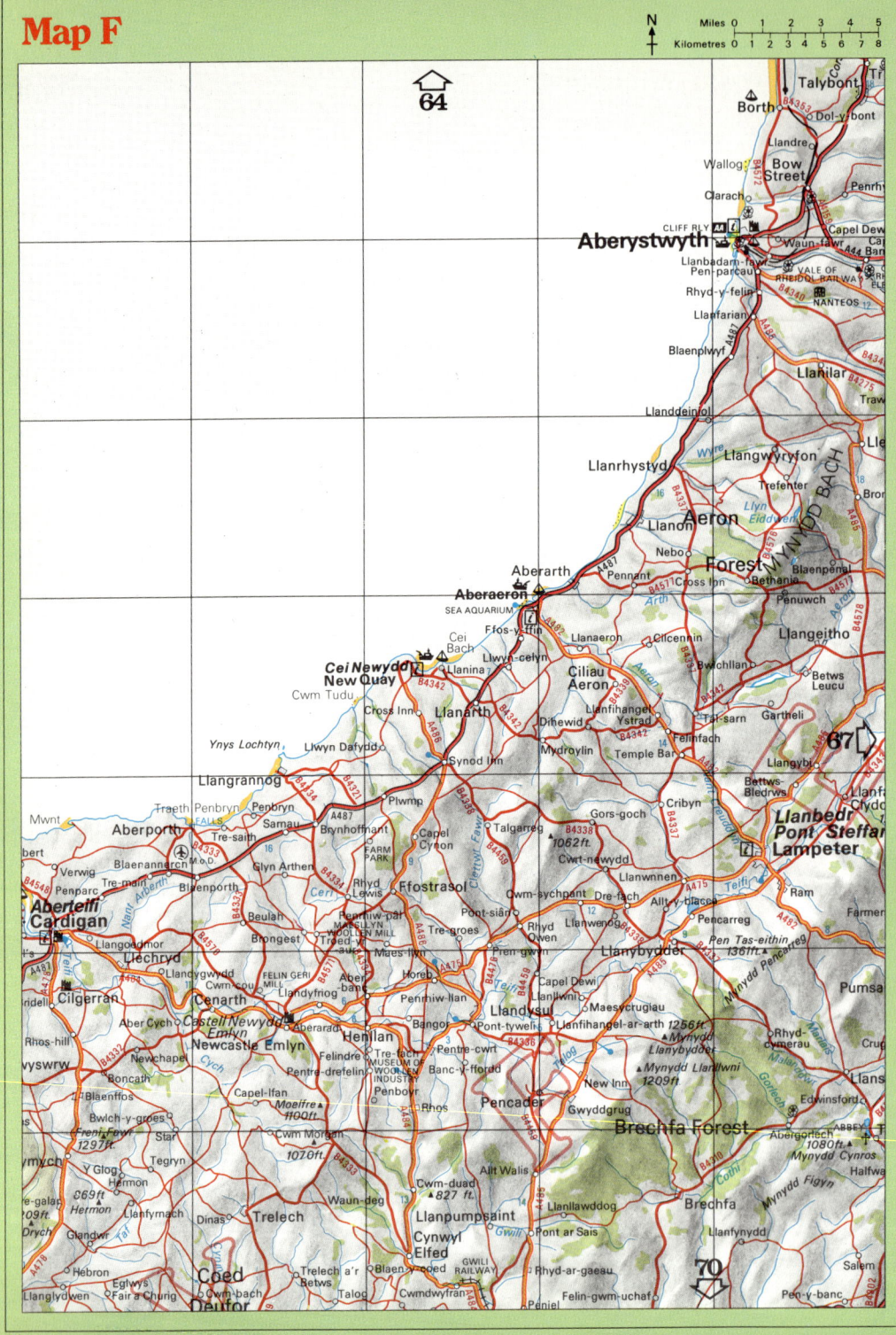

Map F

N

| Miles | 0 | 1 | 2 | 3 | 4 | 5 |
| Kilometres | 0 | 1 | 2 | 3 | 4 | 5 | 6 | 7 | 8 |

Elerch
Disgwylfa Fawr 1661ft.
Drum Peithnant
Tor Du 1659ft.
Y Foel 1791ft.
Llanidloes
Coed-y-gaer 1183ft.
Y Foel 1423ft.
Berth-ddu
Llyn-dwr Hill
GLYNDWR
Pen-Bwlch-y-groes 1487ft.
Cwm-belan
Rhydd Hywel 1920ft.
Moel
65
Eisteddfa-gurig
Dyffryn Castell
Ponterwyd
1398ft.
Old Chapel Hill
Moel
Llanbadarn Fynydd

Ystwyth Forest
Llangurig
Pistyll
Dulas
Pen-rhyn-coch
Dewi Capel Bangor
Goginan
BWLCH NANT YR ARIAN FOREST VISITOR CENTRE
LLYWERNOG SILVER LEAD MINE
Bryn Garw 2003ft.
1870ft.
Cefn Cenarth 1508ft.
Dyrysgol
Pantydwr
Bwlch-y-sarnau
St. Harmon
Moel Hywel
Wenallt 1546ft.
Llanano
ROOD SCREEN
RHEIDOL HYDRO ELECTRIC SCHEME
Devil's Bridge
Ysbyty Cynfyn
1183ft.
Yr Allt
ABBEY CWMHIR
Llanb
Llanfihangel-y-creuddyn
Cnwch-coch
Cyrnau Bach 1271ft.
Esgair Elan
Aber-gwngy
Gamallt
Coed Sarnau
Llanwrthwl
Ddol
Trawsgoed
Llanafan
Cwm Ystwyth
1873ft.
Geifes
Pant Llwyd 1798ft.
Craig-nach Resr.
Gwynllyn
Rhaeadr Rhayader
Gaufron
Cross Gates
Fron
Lledrod
Mynydd Bach
Ysbyty Ystwyth
FALLS
Trumau
Llansantffraid Cwmdeuddwr
Nant-glas
Nant-gwared
A44
Nantmel
Gwystre
Ystrad Meurig
Ffair-rhos
Llyn Teifi
Pontrhydfendigaid
Dibyn Du
STRATA FLORIDA ABBEY
1738ft.
Claerwen Resr.
Garreg-ddu Resr.
1668ft. Esgair Garthen
Elan
Corn Gafallt 1530ft.
Llanfihangel Helygen
Llandrindod Wells
SPA
Bronant
Swydd-y-ffynnon
Cors Goch Glanteifi
Pen-y-bwlch 1649ft.
Pen Maen-wern
Cahan-coch
Doldowlod
Llanyre
Howey
Carn Gron 1777ft.
Bryn Garw 1827ft.
1784ft.
Y Gamriw 1968ft.
Drum Ddu 1761ft.
66
Tregaron
Drum Ddu 1668ft.
Cefn Cnwc 1728ft.
Drum Eira 1968ft.
Drygarn Fawr 2104ft.
Gorllwyn 2009ft.
Newbridge on Wye
Disserth
Crossway
Bettws Disserth
Bryn Rhudd 1574ft.
Esgair Berwyn
1732ft.
Llanfihangel Bryn Pabuan
Llanafan Fawr
Cymbach
Llansaintffraed in Elvel
Tywi Forest
Llanddewi Brefi
Esgair Llethr 1543ft.
Cefn Coch 1642ft.
Llanerch-yrfa
Pen Carreg-dan 1620ft.
Pentre
Llwyn'rllwyd
Builth Road
68
Llethr Llwyd 1524ft.
Maes-glas
Pen-y-gurnos 1498ft.
Abergwesyn
Llwyn Madoc
1516ft.
Cefn Crug
Beulah
Cefn Funog 1476ft.
Cefn-y-bedd
Llanafan-fechan
Llanfaredd
Bryn Rhyd 1588ft.
Bryn Brawd
Soar-y-mynydd
Llyn Brianne
Irfon Forest
Garth
CAMBRIAN WOOLLEN MILL
Llanfair-ym-Muallt Builth Wells
Llanddewi Cwm
Llanbadarn-y
Carn Nant-yr-ast
1279ft.
1445ft.
Cefn Gwenffrwd
1695ft.
Mynydd Trawsnant
Moelfre 1446ft.
Alltmawr 1550ft.
Banc-y-celyn
Aberedw
Llandeilo-gra
Llanwrtyd Wells
Llangammarch Wells
Llandeilo'r Fan
Llanddewi Cwm
Rhandirmwyn
Mynydd Mallaen 1471ft.
Crychan Forest
Drum Ddu 1554ft.
Cwm Owen
Gwenddwr
Crickadarn
Erw
Caeo Forest
Llandre
FALLS
Calycwm
Caio
Cefn Llwydlo 1175ft.
Llandulas
MYNYDD EPPYNT
Bryn Du 1554ft.
Cefn Clawdd 1261ft.
Upper Chapel
Brycheiniog Forest
Crugybar
Porth-y-rhyd
Ffrwd
Cilycwm
Cyngnordy
Gwrhyd 1485ft.
Ysgwydd Hwch 1495ft.
Llandefalle Hill
Llys
Lower Chapel
Llandefalle
Noethgrug 1347ft.
Llandeilo'r Fan
Llanfihangel Nant Bran
Merthyr Cynog
Pont-faen
Palachddu
Llanwrda
Llandovery
Llanymddyfri
Plas Glansevin
WELSH EVENINGS
Halfway
Pentre-bach
Trallong
Penpont
Llandefaelog Fach
Penywre Llandew
Tre-don
Talley
Llangadog
Myddfai
Mynydd Myddfai
Llywel
Pentre'r-felin
Trecastle
Aberyscir
GAER
Aberhonddu Brecon
Felindre
Manordeilo
Bethlehem
Pont Aber
Mynydd Wysg
Defynnog
Sennybridge
MOUNTAIN CENTRE
Llanfrynach
Llandeilo
Capel Gwynfe
Rhiwiau
Twynllannan
Glasfynydd Forest
Mynydd Wysg
Crai
Moel Feity 1940ft.
Heol Senni
Libanus
Mynydd Illtyd
Cantref
Pencelli
Rhosmaen
Llanddeusant
Cefn Cul 1844ft.
Fan Frynych 1980ft.
Allt Ddu 1845ft.
Bryn 1842ft.
Talybont on Usk
Llandeilo
Ffair-fach
Cefn y Truman
MOUNTAIN
BRECON BEACONS
Brycheiniog Fan 2630ft.
238ft.
Fan Fawr 2409ft.
2176ft.
BRECON BEACONS
Pen-y-fan 2907ft.
2502ft.
Gwaun-rhudd
Aber
Talybont
Llyn y Fan Fawr
FFOREST FAWR
Cray Resr.
Chwefr
Fan Llia
Neuadd Resrs.
Storey Arms

67

Map H

65

Black Mountain 1469ft.
GLYNDWR'S WAY
Bryn Gydfa 1573ft. Felindre
Moel Wilym 1568ft.
Beguildy
lanbadarn Eynydd
Black Mt.
Duthlas
Llanfair Waterdine
Beacon Hill 1796ft.
Source of R. Lugg
Aston
Craven Arms 54
Clun
Bromfield
Ludlow
A49
A4112
A4113
Leintwardine

WOOD GREEN
Bryn-melyn
Llanbister
Aran
Knucklas
Bailey Hill
Crug
Llangunllo
Banpunton
Tref-y-Clawdd Knighton
OFFA'S DYKE CENTRE
OFFA'S DYKE HILL
B4355
B4356
B4357
B4358

Llanddewi Ystradenny
Bleddfa
Glog Hill 1335ft.
Rhos-y-meirch
Pilleth
Llanwen Hill
Wigmore
Richards Castle
Woofferton
A456

Radnor Forest
Whitton
Norton
Lugg

Dolau
Penybont
Bach Hill 2002ft.
Radnor Forest
Kinnerton
Discoed
Presteigne
Mortimer's Cross
Luston
Leominster
A44
A4110

Llandegley
Llanfihangel Rhydithon
Evenjobb
Maes Treylow
B4362
B4357

New Radnor
Waiton
Eardisland
A4112
A44

Little Hill 1532ft.
Llanfihangel Nant Melan
Gwaunceste Hill 1778ft.
Gladestry
Old Radnor
Dolyhir
Gwaithla
Kington
Lyonshall
Weobley
Bush Bank
Bodenham Moor
A417

67

Red Hill 1666ft.
Colva Hill
Colfa
Glascwm
Hundred House
Newchurch
Brilley Mountain
Michaelchurch on Arrow
Eardisley
HEREFORD AND
Sutton St. Nicholas

badarn garreg
Bryngwyn 1532ft.
Llanbedr Hill
Rhos-goch
Clyro Hill 1533ft.
Rhydspence
Willersley
WORCESTER
Lugwardine
A438

landeilo Hill
B4594
Painscastle
Clifford
Bronydd
Wye
Clyro
Hereford
A465
A4103

twood
Llanstephan
Llowes
Hay-on-Wye
Madley
Wye

Boughrood
Glasbury
Llanigon
Vowchurch
Kingstone
Callow
Much Dewchurch
A49

Llyswen
Aberllynfi Three Cocks
Hay Bluff 2220ft.
Lord Hereford's Knob 2263ft.
Llaneleu
GOLDEN VALLEY
A465

Bronllys
ROMANY HOLIDAY CARAVAN SITE
Talgarth
Honddu
Wormbridge
A465

Llanfilo
Tretecs
Pengenffordd
Wsun Fach 2660ft.
Pen-y-beacon-fawr 2624ft.
BLACK
† PRIORY
Llanvihangel
Crucorney
Grosmont
Sandyway
A466

Llanfihangel Tal-y-llyn
Llangorse
Llan-gors Lake
Mynydd Du
MOUNTAINS 2504ft.
Pen-twyn-mawr
Forest
Crug Mawr 1805ft.
Cwmyoy
Pandy
Llangattock Lingoed
Cross Ash
Ynysgynwraidd Skenfrith
Llangrove

Scethrog
Cathedine
Cwmdu
Pencerrig-calch Partrishow
WOOD GREEN
Llanfihangel Crucorney
White Castle
Newcastle
Maypole
Whitchurch
A4231

Bwlch
Tretower 2301ft.
Llanbedr
Sugar Loaf Betws 1955ft.
Skirrid-fawr 1596ft.
Llanvetherine
Rockfield
B4233
B4347

77
Coed-yr-ynys
Crickhowell
Llangynidr
Llangattock
Llangrwyne
Mardy

Map J

70

PEMBROKESHIRE COAST NATIONAL PARK

Car Ferry Rosslare-Fishguard

Cardigan Island
Cemaes Hd.
Pen-yr-afr
Mwnt
Gwbert
Poppit Sands
ABBEY
Aber
Car

St. Dogmael's
Llandudoch
Moylgrove
Trewyddel
Ceibwr
Llanrhyd
Glan-rhyd
Bridell
Nanhyfer
Nevern
Rhos-
Felindre-Farchog
Eglwyswr

Strumble Head
Carreg Wastad Pt.
Pwll Gwaelod
Dinas Head
wm-yr-eglwys
Trwyn y Bwa
Newport Bay
Parrog
Trefdraeth
Newport
Pen Brush
Pen Caer
Llanwnda
Fishguard
Bay
Aber Bach
Dinas
Nevern
Carningli Common
PENTRE IFAN
Ffynnongroes

Pen
Goodwick
Abergwaun
Fishguard
Manorowen
Llanlawer
1008ft.
Mynydd Melyn
1021 ft.
Mynydd Caregog
Brynberian
Crymych

Tref asser
Tremarchog
St. Nicholas
Aber-bach
Aber-mawr
Pen Morfa
Granston
Jordanston
Scleddau
Llanychaer
GWAUN VALLEY
Pontfaen
MYNYDD PRESELI

Abercastle
Mathry
Trecwn
1096ft.
Mynydd Cilciffeth
1535ft.
Foel Eryr
1760ft.
Mynydd
Castlebythe
Foel Cwm-cerwyn
1209ft.
Foel Drych

Pen Clegyr
Porthgain
Castle Morris
Cas-mael
Puncheston
1137ft.
Motel
Resr.
Coed
Rosebush
Mynachlog-ddu

Aber Eiddi
Llanrhian
Trefin
Tretetert
Letterston
Castlebythe
Preseli
Henry's
Moat
Maenclochog
Llangly

St. David's Head
Croes-goch
Tretio
Llanreithan
Ces-newydd Bach
Little Newcastle
Tufton
Clyn
New Moat
Llangly

Whitesand Bay
Caerfarchell
Llanhowel
Newton
Wolf's castle
Hayscastle Cross
Woodstock
Llys-y-fran
Llan-y-cefn
Login

Ramsey Island
Rhodiad
Whitchurch
Middle Mill
Hayscastle
Treffgarne
R.A.F.
Ambleston
Cilymaenllwyd
Llandvsilio

St. David's
Caerbwdi
Solfach
Brawdy
583ft.
Dudwell Mt.
Trefgarn
Spital
Walton East
Pen-ffordd
Bletherston
Llanfa

CHAPEL
Porthclais
Clegyr Berfai
Dinas Fawr
Green
Scar
Solva
Niwgwl
Newgale
Roch
Woltsdale
Scolton
Rudbaxton
WITHYBUSH AIRFIELD
Clarbeston
Clarbeston Road
Wiston
Clunderwen
Castelldwyran
Rh

NECTARIUM
Simpson Cross
Camrose
Egremont
Llanfa

Rickets Head
Nolton
Keeston
Pelcomb Br.
Crundale
Clawhaden
Llanddewi Vel
Login

St. BRIDE'S BAY
Druidston
Haroldston West
Lambston
Portfield Gate
Dreenhill
Hwlffordd
Haverfordwest
Robeston Wathen
Redstone Bank
Narberth
Lampet

Broad Haven
Broadway
Radford Br.
The Rhos
Slebech
Minwear
Coed
Prince's Gate
Tavernspi

Little Haven
Walton West
GRAHAM SUTHERLAND ART GALLERY
Landshipping
Preseli
Templeton
Ludchurch
Crun

Talbenny
Rosepool
Hasguard
Walwyn's
Castle
Tiers
Cross
Freystrop
Hook
Martletwy
Yerbeston
Begelly
Reynalton
Stepaside

The Nab Head
St. Brides
Musselwick Sands
Johnston
Sardis
Llangwm
Cresswell
Jeffreston
Hill
Broadmoor
Kilgety
Wiser

Garland Stone
Marloses Sands
Westdale
Marloses
Sandy Haven
Herbrandston
Milford Haven
Millfwrd
Houghton
Lawrenny
Cresswell
Redberth
Williamston
Saunder

Skomer Island
Gelliswick
Bay
Waterston
Neyland
Burton
Cosheston
Carew
Sageston
New Hedges
Dinb
Tenb

Mew Stone
Gateholm
St. Ishmael's
Dale
Doc Penfro
Pembroke Dock
Pentro
Williamston
B4318
St. Florence
Gumfreston
Penally

BROAD SOUND
Skokholm Island
Thorn
Island
Angle
Rhoscrowther
Pembroke
MILITARY
Milton
Carew
Cheriton
MANOR HOUSE LEISURE PARK
St. Catherine
Caldy Sd.

St. Ann's Head
Sheep Island
Pwllcrochan
Hundleton
BISHOPS PALACE
Lamphey
Jameston
Lydstep
Giltar Pt.

MILFORD HAVEN
Freshwater West
Newton
Maiden Wells
Kingston
Freshwater
Hodgeston
Cheriton
Swanlake
Manorbier
MONA
Caldy

PEMBROKESHIRE
Castlemartin
Orielton
St. Petrox
Trewent Pt.
Old Castle Hd.

Linney Head
Warren
Merrion
Bosherston
Stackpole
Barafundle Bay

Stack Rocks
CHAPEL
Saddle Hd.
St. Govan's Head
Stackpole Head
Broad Haven

COAST NATIONAL PARK

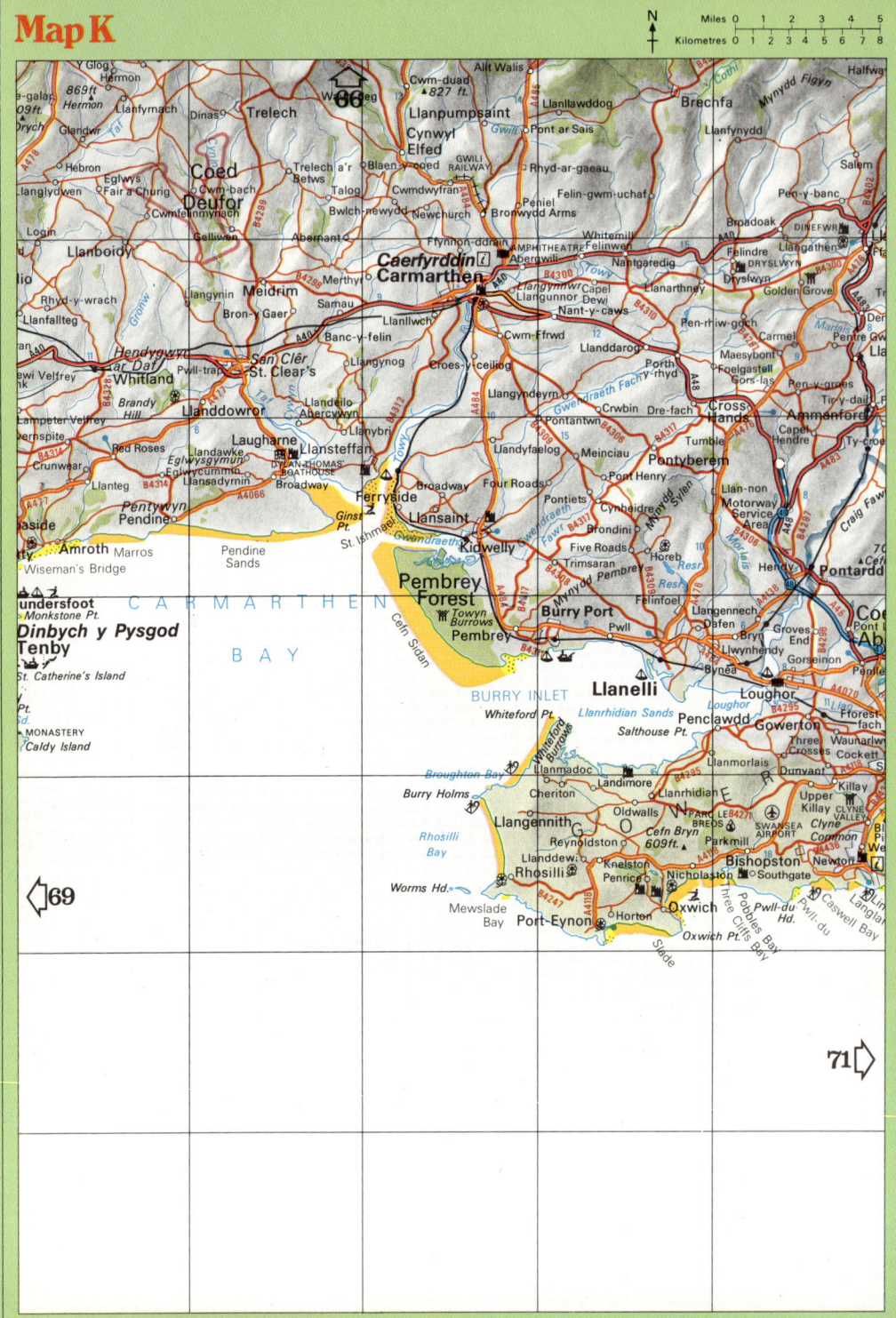

Miles 0 1 2 3 4 5
Kilometres 0 1 2 3 4 5 6 7 8

Y Glog
Hermon
869ft
Hermon
Llanfyrnach
Dinas
Trelech
66
Cwm-duad
Allt Walis
Brechfa
Mynydd Figyn
Halfwa
-galar
09ft.
rych
Glandwr
Llanpumpsaint
Cynwyl Elfed
Llanllawddog
Pont ar Sais
Llanfynydd
Coed Deufor
Hebron
Eglwys Fair a Churig
Cwm-bach
Cwmfelinmynach
Trelech a'r Betws
Blaen-y-coed
Talog
GWILI RAILWAY
Rhyd-ar-gaeau
Peniel
Felin-gwm-uchaf
Pen-y-banc
Salem
Login
Abernant
Cwmdwyfran
Newchurch
Bronwydd Arms
Broadoak
DINEFWR
Llanboidy
io
Rhyd-y-wrach
Llangynin
Meidrim
Merthyr
Flynnon-ddrain
Caerfyrddin
Carmarthen
Aberdwili
Felinwen
Whitmill
Nantgaredig
Felindre
Capel Dewi
DRYSLWYN
Dryslwyn
Broadoak
Golden Grove
Llanfallteg
Bron-y Gaer
Samau
Llanllwch
Llangynnwr
Llangunnor
Nant-y-caws
Llanarthney
ewi Velfrey
Hendygwyn ar Daf
Whitland
San Clêr
St. Clear's
Banc-y-felin
Llangynog
Croes-y-ceiling
Cwm-Ffrwd
Llanddarog
Porth-y-rhyd
Carmel
Maesybont
Foelgastell
Pen-y-groes
Cross Hands
Ammanford
Lampeter Velfrey
vernspite
Brandy Hill
Llanddowror
Llandeilo Abercywyn
Red Roses
Laugharne
Llansteffan
Llanybri
Llandyfaelog
Meinciau
Pontyberem
Llan-non
Motorway Service Area
Craig Faw
Crunwear
Llanteg
Eglwyscummin
Lansadyrnin
DYLAN THOMAS BOATHOUSE
Broadway
Broadway
Four Roads
Pontiets
Cynheidre
Pont Henry
Brondini
aside
Pentywyn
Pendine
St. Ishmael
Ferryside
Llansaint
Gwendraeth
Kidwelly
Five Roads
Horeb
Resr
Pontardd
Amroth
Marros
Wiseman's Bridge
Pendine Sands
Ginst Pt.
Trimsaran
Mynydd Pembrey
Hendy
undersfoot
Monkstone Pt.
Dinbych y Pysgod
Tenby
CARMARTHEN
Cefn Sidan
Pembrey Forest
Towyn Burrows
Pembrey
Burry Port
Felinfoel
Llangennech
Dafen
Bryn
Groves End
Llwynhendy
Gorseinon
Pont
Ab
Coe
St. Catherine's Island
BAY
Pwll
Bynea
69
MONASTERY
Caldy Island
BURRY INLET
Whiteford Pt.
Llanrhidian Sands
Salthouse Pt.
Llanelli
Penclawdd
Loughor
Gowerton
Three Crosses
Waunarlw
Cockett
Loughor
Forest fach
Pt.
Sd.
Llanmorlais
Dunvant
R
Killay
Broughton Bay
Llanmadoc
Cheriton
Landimore
Llanrhidian
Parc
BREOS
Upper Killay
CLYNE
VALLEY
Burry Holms
Oldwalls
G
SWANSEA AIRPORT
Clyne Common
Bi
Rhosilli Bay
Langennith
Reynoldston
Cefn Bryn
609ft.
Parkmill
Three Crosses
Bishopston
Newton
Llanddewi
Rhosilli
Knelston
Penrice
Nicholaston
Southgate
Worms Hd.
Mewslade Bay
Port-Eynon
Horton
Oxwich
Oxwich Pt.
Three Cliffs Bay
Slade
Pwll-du Hd.
Caswell Bay
Langla
Pobbles Bay
71

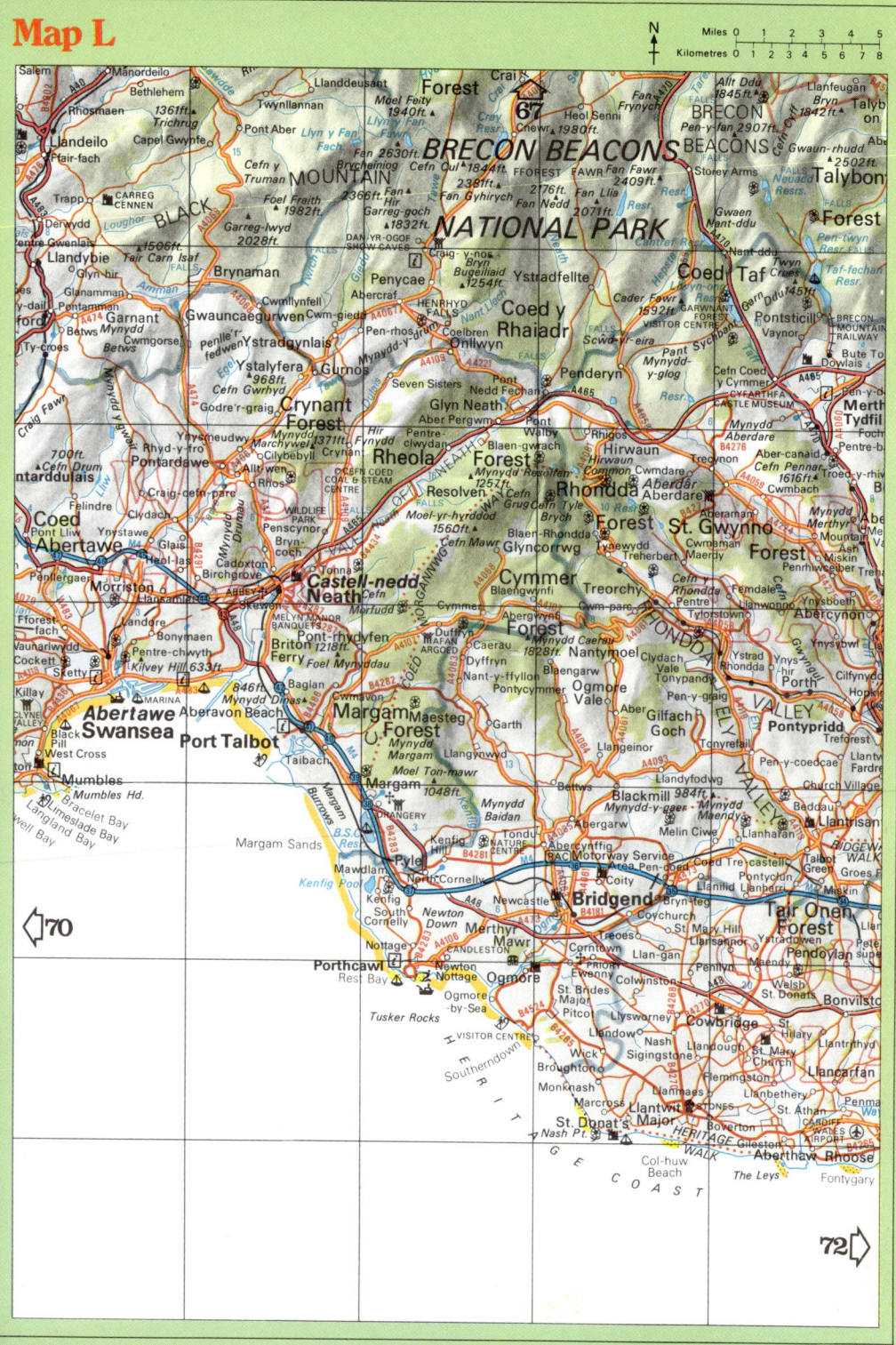

Map L

N

Salem · Manordeilo
Bethlehem
Rhosmaen · 1361ft. Trichrug
Llandeilo · Twynllannan
Ffair-fach · Capel Gwynfe
Pont Aber
Trapp · CARREG CENNEN

Llanddeusant
Moel Feity 1940ft.
Llyn y Fan Fach
Cefn y Fan 2630ft.
Truman MOUNTAIN · Brycheiniog 1844ft.
Foel Fraith · Fan 2366ft. 1982ft.
Garreg-goch · Fan Gyhirych 2381ft. 2276ft. Fan Nedd 2071ft.
Garreg-lwyd 2028ft.

BRECON BEACONS
Cefn Cul FOREST FAWR Fan Fawr 2409ft.

Crai
Cefn y FOREST
Cray Fan Frynych

67
Heol Senni
Pen-y-fan 2907ft.
Fan Llia

Allt Ddu 1845ft.
Llanfeugan
Bryn 1842ft. Talybon
BRECON
BEACONS Gwaun-rhudd 2502ft. Storey Arms Resr. Neuadd Resrs. Talybont
Allt-ma

NATIONAL PARK
Gwaen
Nant-ddu

Forest
Pen-twyn
Resr.

Black
MOUNTAIN
Brynaman
Penycae · Bryn
DAN-YR-OGOF
SHOW CAVES
Craig-y-nos
Bugeiliaid 1254ft.
Ystradfellte

Coed Taf
Resr.
Twyn
Taf-fechan
Resr.

Llandybie · Tair Carn Isaf 1506ft.
Glyn-hir
Glanamman · Pontamman · A474
Garnant Mynydd
Betws Cwmgorse
Gwauncaegurwen
Cwmllynfell
Abercraf
Cwm-gied A4067
HENRHYD
FALLS
Penrhos
Coelbren
Onllwyn

Cader Fawr 1592ft.
Scwd-yr-eira
GARWNANT
FOREST
VISITOR CENTRE
Pontsticill
Vaynor

Coed y Rhaiadr
Penderyn

Cefn Coed
y Cymmer
Merthyr
Tydfil
Bute to
Dowlais

CYFARTHFA
CASTLE MUSEUM

Ty-croes
Cwmgorse
Ystradgynlais
penlle'r
fedwen
Gurnos 968ft.
Ystalyfera
Cefn Gwrhyd
Godre'r-graig

Pont
Nedd Fechan
Walby
Rhigos
Hirwaun
Common
Aber Pergwm
Glyn Neath
Pont

Hirwaun
Penrhiw

Mynydd
y-glog

Mynydd
Aberdare

Cefn-canaidd
1616ft.
Cefn Pennar
Cwmbach

Pont Sychnant

Mynydd
Merthyr
Miskin

Crynant
Forest
Rheola
Forest

Hir Fynydd
Cefn-
clwydau

Blaen-gwrach
Resolven
Cefn Tyle
Brych

Rhondda
Aberdare
Aberaman
St. Gwynno
Forest

Coed Liw
Abertawe

Pontardawe
Clydach
Glais
Birchgrove

Ynysmeudwy
Marchywel 971ft.
Clybebyll
Alltwen
Rhos

Moel-yr-hyrddod 1560ft.
Grug Cefn
Tyle

Cefn Mawr
Blaen-Rhondda
Gyfeillion
Treherbert
Maerdy

Treorchy

Castell-nedd
Neath

Tonna
Cefn

Forest
Blaengwynfi
Cwmparc
Pentre
Tylorstown
Ynysboeth
Abercynon
Ynysybwl

Abertawe
Swansea
Port Talbot

Cymmer
Treorchy

70

Margam
Forest
Maesteg
Garth
Gilfach
Goch
Pontypridd

Porthcawl
Ogmore
Bridgend
Tair Onen
Forest
Pendoylan

Cowbridge
Llancarfan

Aberthaw
Rhoose

72

Miles 0 1 2 3 4 5
Kilometres 0 1 2 3 4 5 6 7 8

Cwmdu
Llansantffraid
Bwlch
Crug Mawr
1805ft.
Talybont
on Usk
Pencerrig-calch Partrishow
HOOD
SCREEN
Pandy
Ynysgynwraidd
Skenfrith
Llangrove
Aber
Coed-yr-ynys
Tretower 230ft.
Llanbedr
Llanfihangel
Crucorney
Craig
Serethin
Llangattock
Lingoed
Cross Ash
Maypole
Whitchurch
2ft.
Talybont
Rest
Brecon
Sugar Loaf Betws
1955ft.
Skirrid-fawr
1596ft.
68
Llanvetherine
Newcastle
B4347
Rockfield
Llangynidr
Crickhowell
Llangattock
WHITE CASTLE
Pentre
Trefynwy
Monmouth
Garn Caws
1692ft.
Mynydd Llangynidr
1805ft.
Clydach
Gilwern
Y Fenni
Abergavenny
Croes
Mardy
Llantilio
Crossenny
Over Monnow
WYE
Trefil
Resr.
Blackrock
Govilon
Llanddewi
Rhydderch
Llanvapley
Wern-y-heolydd
Wonastow
Mitchel
Troy
Penallt
Newland
Brynmawr
Beaufort
Llanfoist
1833ft.
Borenge
Llanellen
Llanarth
Tregaer
Bryn-gwyn
Dingestow
Cwmcarvan
Whitebrook
Dukestown
Sirhowy
Newtown
Nant-y-glo
Coalbrookvale
BIG PIT
MINING
MUSEUM
Blaenafon
Llanover
Llangattock
nigh Usk
Raglan
Pen-y-clawdd
Trelech
Tintern
Tredegar
Ebbw
Vale
Blaina
Llanvapley
Mynydd
Garn-clochdy
Bettws-newydd
Kingcoed
Llanishen
Parkhouse
Llandogo
Rhymney
Pontlottyn
Cwm
Cwm-tillery
Mynydd
Commander
Kemeys
Commander
Llancayo
Llansoy
Trelech Grange
VALLEY
Tintern
New
Tredegar
Abertillery
Abersychan
Mamhilad
Penperlleni
Monkswood
Gwernesney
Usk
Llangwm
Wolves
Newton
FOLK
CENTRE
Devauden
Chepstow
Park Wood
St. Arvans
RACE
COURSE
Bargoed
Six Bells
Llanhilleth
Glascoed
Llandegfedd
Reservoir
Llanbadoc
Common
Coed-y-paen
Llanllywel
Newchurch
Cas-gwent
Chepstow
Pwll-Meyric
Ystrad
Mynach
Ebbw
Forest
Pont-newydd
Upper
Cwmbran
Llangybi
Llantrisant
Mynydd Badh
Senghenydd
Maes-y-cwmmer
Ynys-ddu
Cwm-carn
FOREST
DRIVE
Cross Keys
Llanfrechfa
Fredunnock
Pont-
hir
Llanhennock
Wentwood
Shirenewton
Wentwood
Reservoir
CHAPEL
Caerwent
Mathern
Caerphilly
Rudry
Machen
Lower
Machen
Rogerstone
14
LOCKS
Pentre-poeth
Bettws
Caerleon
AMPHITHEATRE
RAC
Christchurch
Llanmartin
St. Pride's
Netherwent
NEW
MANOR
WALK
Caerwent
Crick
Portskewett
Clifton
Sudbrook
Bedwas
Thornhill
Bassaleg
Casnewydd
Newport
Bishton
Magor
Undy
Rogiet
Redwick
Tongwynlais
Llanedeyrn
Castleton
Marshfield
Nash
Whitson
Goldcliff
AVONMOUTH
Whitchurch
St. Mellons
Rumney
Peterstone Wentlloog
SEVERN ESTUARY
Cardiff
Caerdydd
Cardiff
Docks
Clevedon
AVON
Penarth
Nailsea
Dinas
Powys
Lavernock
Ranny Bay
Lavernock Pt.
Barry
Sully Island
PLEASURE PARK HOLIDAY CAMP
Flat Holm
Weston
-super-Mare
The Knap
Barry Island
Whitmore Bay
Steep Holme
Blagdon

71